1 MONTH OF
FREE
READING

at

www.ForgottenBooks.com

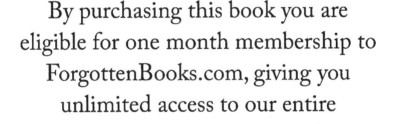

By purchasing this book you are eligible for one month membership to ForgottenBooks.com, giving you unlimited access to our entire collection of over 1,000,000 titles via our web site and mobile apps.

To claim your free month visit:

www.forgottenbooks.com/free305077

ISBN 978-0-428-19750-6
PIBN 10305077

Issued April 2, 1908.

U. S. DEPARTMENT OF AGRICULTURE,

BUREAU OF CHEMISTRY—BULLETIN No. 108.

H. W. WILEY, Chief of Bureau.

COMMERCIAL FEEDING STUFFS OF THE UNITED STATES:

THEIR CHEMICAL AND MICROSCOPICAL EXAMINATION.

BY

J. K. HAYWOOD,
Chief, Miscellaneous Laboratory,

AND

H. J. WARNER,
Assistant Chemist, Miscellaneous Laboratory,

WITH THE COLLABORATION OF

B. J. HOWARD,
Chief, Microchemical Laboratory.

WASHINGTON:
GOVERNMENT PRINTING OFFICE.
1908.

Issued April 2, 1908.

U. S. DEPARTMENT OF AGRICULTURE,

BUREAU OF CHEMISTRY—BULLETIN No. 108.

H. W. WILEY, Chief of Bureau.

COMMERCIAL FEEDING STUFFS OF THE UNITED STATES:

THEIR CHEMICAL AND MICROSCOPICAL EXAMINATION.

BY

J. K. HAYWOOD,
Chief, Miscellaneous Laboratory,

AND

H. J. WARNER,
Assistant Chemist, Miscellaneous Laboratory,

WITH THE COLLABORATION OF

B. J. HOWARD,
Chief, Microchemical Laboratory.

WASHINGTON:

GOVERNMENT PRINTING OFFICE.

1908.

LETTER OF TRANSMITTAL.

UNITED STATES DEPARTMENT OF AGRICULTURE,
BUREAU OF CHEMISTRY,
Washington, D. C., August 27, 1907.

SIR: I have the honor to submit for your approval a report giving the results obtained in an investigation, of the composition of commercial feeding stuffs sold on the American market, which has been made in the miscellaneous laboratory of this Bureau, according to law. The investigation was undertaken in order that we might efficiently answer the many inquiries received at the Bureau for information regarding this class of goods. As the results are of general interest, I recommend that the report be published as Bulletin 108 of the Bureau of Chemistry.

Respectfully,
W. D. BIGELOW,
Acting Chief of Bureau.

Hon. JAMES WILSON,
Secretary of Agriculture.

2

CONTENTS.

3

ILLUSTRATIONS.

a On Plates V and VI the name Decaisne is by mistake printed "Ducaisne."

6

COMMERCIAL FEEDING STUFFS OF THE UNITED STATES: THEIR CHEMICAL AND MICROSCOPICAL EXAMINATION.

INTRODUCTION.

Extensive investigations on commercial feeding stuffs have been conducted by a number of experiment stations, in connection with the enforcement of the feeding-stuff laws in the various States. These laws, however, usually require a guaranty as to fat and protein only, and consequently the examinations by the stations have been in most cases limited to these two constituents. In a few cases determinations have also been made by the stations of ash, crude fiber, and nitrogen-free extract by difference, but practically no attempt has been made to determine any of the various carbohydrates that constitute the so-called nitrogen-free extract.

From a scientific as well as practical point of view a more complete analysis seemed desirable, as such data would give a better idea of the true composition of a stock food, and thus make possible a fairer comparison of the relative feeding values of the different varieties.

In addition to the chemical analyses, a microscopical examination of the stock foods was made by B. J. Howard, chief of the microchemical laboratory, and his report is appended.

CHEMICAL EXAMINATION.

COLLECTION OF SAMPLES.

During the spring of 1904, arrangements were made with the experiment stations of New York and Massachusetts whereby their representatives sent samples of the various stock foods collected by them to this Bureau. Several hundred samples were sent and upon receipt were carefully bottled and corked. If they contained an excessive amount of moisture, they were dried in bulk before being bottled. A small amount of the original sample was reserved for microscopical examination, the remainder being ground fine, passed through a sieve with circular holes 1 millimeter in diameter, and rebottled.

METHODS OF ANALYSIS.

In the analysis of these foods, the following determinations were made: Moisture, ash, ether extract, crude protein, crude fiber, starch, sucrose, reducing sugars, and pentosans. The methods used for moisture, ash, ether extract, crude protein, and crude fiber are the official methods of the Association of Official Agricultural Chemists.[a] The methods for pentosans and starch are those provisionally adopted by this association, and the methods for determining sucrose and reducing sugars those used by the miscellaneous laboratory for determining these constituents in most cattle foods and forage crops. These methods are as follows:

DETERMINATION OF PENTOSANS.

(1) PURIFICATION OF PHLOROGLUCOL.

Heat in a beaker about 300 cc of hydrochloric acid (specific gravity 1.06) and 11 grams of phloroglucol added in small quantities at a time, stirring constantly until it has almost entirely dissolved. Some impurities may resist solution, but it is unnecessary to dissolve them. Pour the hot solution into a sufficient quantity of the same hydrochloric acid (cold) to make the volume 1,500 cc. Allow it to stand at least over night— better several days—to allow the diresorcol to crystallize out, and filter immediately before using. The solution may turn yellow, but this does not interfere with its usefulness. In using it, add the volume containing the required amount to the distillate.

(2) DETERMINATION.

Place a quantity of the material, chosen so that the weight of phloroglucid obtained shall not exceed 0.300 grams, in a flask, together with 100 cc of 12 per cent hydrochloric acid (specific gravity, 1.06) and several pieces of recently heated pumice stone; place the flask upon a wire gauze, connect it with a condenser and apply heat, rather gently at first, and so regulate as to distil over 30 cc in about ten minutes, the distillate passing through a small filter paper. Replace the 30 cc driven over by a like quantity of the dilute acid, added by means of a separatory funnel in such a manner as to wash down the particles adhering to the sides of the flask, and continue the process until the distillate amounts to 360 cc. To the complete distillate gradually add a quantity of phloroglucol (purified if necessary) dissolved in 12 per cent hydrochloric acid, and thoroughly stir the resulting mixture. The amount of phloroglucol used should be about double that of the furfural expected. The solution first turns yellow, then green, and very soon an amorphous greenish precipitate appears, which grows rapidly darker, until it finally becomes almost black. Make the solution up to 400 cc with 12 per cent hydrochloric acid and allow to stand over night.

Filter the amorphous black precipitate into a tared gooch crucible through an asbestos felt, wash carefully with 150 cc of water in such a way that the water is not entirely removed from the crucible until the very last. Then dry for four hours at the temperature of boiling water, cool and weigh in a weighing bottle, the increase in weight being reckoned as phloroglucid. To calculate the furfural, pentoses, or pentosans from the phloroglucid, use the following formulas:

For weight of phloroglucid (a) under 0.03 gram:

$$\text{Furfural} = (a + 0.0052) \times 0.5170$$
$$\text{Pentoses} = (a + 0.0052) \times 1.0170$$
$$\text{Pentosans} = (a + 0.0052) \times 0.8949$$

---

[a] U. S. Dept. Agr., Bureau of Chemistry, Bul. 107, p. 57.

For weight of phloroglucid (a) from 0.03 gram to 0.300 gram Kröber's table[a] is recommended. If this is not available use the following formulas:

$$Furfural = (a+0.0052) \times 0.5185$$
$$Pentoses = (a+0.0052) \times 1.0075$$
$$Pentosans = (a+0.0052) \times 0.8866$$

For weights of phloroglucid (a) over 0.300 gram.

$$Furfural = (a+0.0052) \times 0.5180$$
$$Pentoses = (a+0.0052) \times 1.0026$$
$$Pentosans = (a+0.0052) \times 0.8824$$

DETERMINATION OF REDUCING SUGARS AND SUCROSE.

Weigh 13.2 grams into a 200 cc flask, add about 150 cc water, and shake occasionally for one hour. Add 5 cc alumina cream and make up to 200 cc with water, shake, and filter off 100 cc into a 110 cc flask. Make up to the 110 cc mark with lead sub-acetate, shake, and filter through a folded filter into a small Erlenmeyer flask. If the solution is cloudy return to filter, until a clear filtrate is obtained. This is solution "A."

REDUCING SUGARS AS DEXTROSE.

To 25 cc of solution A add exactly 5 cc of concentrated sodium carbonate solution. Shake and filter through a 9 cm filter into a small flask. Return to filter until a clear filtrate is obtained. Use 20 cc for the determination of dextrose according to Allihn's table (20 cc equals 1 gram of original substance).

SUCROSE.

Transfer 50 cc of solution A to a 55 cc flask and make up to the 55 cc mark with concentrated hydrochloric acid. Mix well and heat in the water bath with bulb of thermometer as near to center of flask as possible until it registers 68° C., taking 15 minutes in the heating. Transfer the solution to a small beaker and neutralize with sodium carbonate. Transfer to a 100 cc flask and make to mark with water. Filter off 25 cc for the determination of total reducing sugars (25 cc equals 0.75 gram of the original substance). Before calculating the invert sugar obtained as sucrose from a table for invert sugar, deduct the reducing sugars, determined as invert sugar from the same table.

The results were first figured on the basis of the sample as received at the laboratory. The sum of the percentages of the different constituents determined does not equal 100 per cent, but the results are as close as can be expected, with the present methods. Factors used for calculation are often of an arbitrary nature, as in the cases of protein and pentosans, and results can not be considered as absolute. Also a number of substances, such as galactan, are not determined. All of the results were refigured to a moisture-free basis.

METHODS OF MANUFACTURE OF STOCK FOODS.

On account of the numerous and varied sources from which the so-called concentrated feed stuffs are derived, it is essential to know something of the raw materials entering into these products and the

[a] Journal für Landwirtschaft, 48, 1900, p. 379; U. S. Dept. Agr., Bureau of Chemistry, Bul. 107, page 226.

manufacturing processes, that the various mixtures may be classified and some idea gained of what their composition should be.

COTTONSEED MEAL.

Cottonseed meal is a by-product from the manufacture of cotton-seed oil. The seeds as they come from the ginning mill are covered with a hard shell and a coating of lint. At the oil mills the fuzzy seeds are subjected to a rough milling for the removal of the black hull and lint. The decorticated seeds are crushed, heated, placed in jute sacks, and subjected to hydraulic pressure, by means of which a portion of the oil is expressed. When the resulting cake is cracked and ground the yellow cottonseed meal of commerce is obtained.

LINSEED MEAL.

At the oil mills the seeds are crushed and then the oil is removed by one of two processes.

In the "old process," the crushed seeds are heated, placed in jute sacks, and subjected to hydraulic pressure. The residue consists of hard slabs or cakes, which are cracked and ground, the product being known as "old process" oil meal.

In the "new process," the crushed seeds are heated and while warm are placed in large vertical percolators, and naphtha or some other volatile solvent is poured over them, which is allowed to drain out at the bottom. This process is repeated until nearly all the oil has been removed. The extracted mass is freed from solvent by letting steam into the percolator and driving out the naphtha as a vapor.

After steaming, the meal is dried, and the resultant by-product is known as "new process" oil meal.

GLUTEN, GLUTEN MEAL, GLUTEN FEED.

These materials are usually obtained as by-products in the manufacture of starch and glucose from corn. The method is practically as follows: The whole corn is soaked for several hours in warm acidified water until soft and swollen. It is then ground in running water and passed through sieves, the starch and part of the gluten passing through, while the husk and germ remain behind. The starch and gluten which are carried by the water are separated from each other by their difference in specific gravity. The by-products are first dried by pressure and then in a kiln. The gluten when sold alone is generally called "gluten meal." More frequently, however, the gluten, husk, and germ are mixed and sold under the name of "gluten feed."

HOMINY FEED.

Hominy, as manufactured for human use, consists of the hard or flinty part of the corn kernel. The hull, germ, and part of the starch portions of the kernel constitute the waste of hominy manufacture. These materials are sold together under the name of hominy chops or feed.

DISTILLERS' DRIED GRAINS.

Distillers' dried grains are a by-product obtained in the manufacture of alcohol or whisky from the cereals. Corn and rye are most often used, sometimes singly, more often in combination. Sometimes certain proportions of oats, wheat, and barley are also added.

The grains are coarsely ground, mixed with water, a malt solution added, and the whole kept at a uniform temperature until most of the starch has changed to sugar. Yeast is then added to convert the sugar to alcohol, which is distilled. The residue from the distillation, or distilling slop, is filtered, dried, and placed on the market as a concentrated food. The dried material, on account of the removal of a large part of the starch and sugar of the grain by the above process, contains an increased percentage of proteids, fat, and crude fiber.

BREWERS' DRIED GRAINS AND MALT SPROUTS.

These are the by-products resulting from malting and brewing processes. The barley is moistened and kept at a warm temperature until the grain germinates. In this process the starch is partially changed to maltose and dextrin. The germinated barley is dried and freed from its sprouts, which are known to commerce as malt sprouts. The malted grains are used in the preparation of the wort in the manufacture of malt liquors. In this process nearly all of the starch of the malt is changed to maltose and dextrin, which are removed in the liquid wort that is subsequently to be used in the preparation of the malt liquor. The residue from this mashing process is kiln-dried and placed upon the market as brewers' dried grains.

It will at once be seen that the sugar and starch content of this product will be very low, while its protein and fat content as well as the amount of other substances present, but not acted upon by the ferment of the malt, will be high.

WHEAT FEEDS.

This term is used to cover any combination of wheat offals or waste products obtained in the manufacture of flour from wheat. Among the products so obtained may be mentioned bran, shorts, middlings, red-dog flour, etc. It is not an easy matter to state just how these various by-products are obtained, nor in fact just what each by-product is, since different writers on the subject seldom exactly agree with one another in the nomenclature employed. The following may be considered as an approximate statement of the process by which these products are obtained during the manufacture of flour. The wheat as it comes to the mill is passed through a series of metallic sieves to remove such products as oats, straw, etc. It is then passed to scourers, where it is well brushed and thus deprived of dust and dirt. After this it is crushed and sifted on coarse bolting cloth. This crushing and sifting is repeated several times and the several siftings not passing through constitute wheat bran. The material that does go through is further pulverized and passed over silk bolting cloth sieves of various degrees of fineness on revolving reels. At the same time it is fanned by currents of air. By this process a fine white flour is finally obtained, the by-products from the process consisting of shorts, the various grades of middlings, red-dog flour, etc. The germ is sometimes removed from the other by-products and used as a breakfast food.

Bran, therefore, consists of the hard outer portions of the wheat kernel, with a little of the starchy portion. Middlings contain the finer bran and more flour particles. Red-dog flour is the lowest grade of flour and is generally of dark color. The term "mixed feed" is generally applied to mixtures of middlings, bran, and the other wheat products, in some instances red-dog flour being also used. Wheat feed is a term often used to cover any combination of wheat offals.

OAT FEEDS.

The main source of oat feeds is the breakfast food factories. In many cases they are composed almost entirely of the oat hulls and light oats left as a waste from oatmeal manufacture. Necessarily these feeds contain a much higher percentage of fiber than whole oats. These materials are often fortified by the use of a nitrogenous concentrate, such as cottonseed meal. Ground whole oats are often used in stock foods, either alone or in combination with other cereals.

CORN AND OAT FEEDS.

Corn and oats ground together in varying porportions are sold under a number of names in different localities. The name "provender" is used in New England to designate a mixture of equal parts of ground oats and corn. "Chop feed" and "corn and oat feed" are also used to designate mixtures of corn and oats. Strictly speaking, these products should be composed of a mixture of ground corn and oats, but often a large proportion of oat hulls are present.

DRIED BEET PULP.

The beets are thoroughly washed, shredded, and placed in a large cylinder; water is admitted and sugar extracted by the diffusion method. After the liquor is withdrawn, the beet pulp is run through a press to remove excess of water. Molasses residues from the sugar factory are thoroughly mixed with beet pulp and the whole kiln dried by direct heat. The resulting dry product is placed on the market as a feeding stuff.

MOLASSES GRAINS.

Molasses residues are added to some dry and bulky material, such as brewer's grains, malt sprouts, oat hulls, or light oats, in such amounts that they are all absorbed. This mixture after drying is known to the trade as "molasses grains."

PROPRIETARY FEEDS.

The proprietary feeds are derived from numerous and varied sources, but very often they serve as the outlet for industrial by-products, such as are obtained in the manufacture of breakfast foods.

ANIMAL MEALS.

Animal meals are of four varieties, as follows: Meat meals, meat and bone meals, bone meals, and blood meals. The meat and bone meals are derived from waste meats, scraps, and bones from the packing houses. They are sold in a dry condition, finely ground. In some cases the bone has been subjected to steam under pressure or kettle rendered, in which case the resulting product is lower both in fat and protein. The blood meals are simply dried blood finely ground and are a by-product of the large packing houses.

POULTRY FOODS.

Poultry foods are composed principally of several cereals, either whole or coarsely ground. Some poultry foods contain also charcoal and ground oyster shells. Other foods of this class are fortified with dried blood, meat scraps, cottonseed or linseed meals. Wheat screenings, containing the small and shriveled wheat and weed seeds, are very often among the chief ingredients.

FOOD VALUES OF THE PRINCIPAL CONSTITUENTS.

A few words in regard to the food value of the principal substances determined may be of interest to those not familiar with the subject. From whatever source feeding stuffs are derived, they owe their nutritive value to three groups of food constituents, namely, proteids, fats, and carbohydrates. Since carbohydrates are contained in abundant quantities in the cheaper, coarse feeds, it is usual to value the more concentrated and higher priced feeds entirely on their protein and fat content. That this does not always give a correct valuation will be shown later.

Protein is of primary importance, as it serves to build up new tissue and replace the broken down cells destroyed in the katabolism of the body. Under certain circumstances, as in starvation, the protein may serve as a source of heat and energy.

Fats are of use principally as sources of heat and energy, being usually reckoned as two and one-fourth times as valuable in this respect as the carbohydrates. They also protect the protein compounds of the body against destruction and serve as a packing and protection for the other tissues.

The carbohydrates are also of importance as sources of heat and energy. The members of this group differ, however, from one another in their nutritive value, since their digestibility varies widely. The starches and sugars are easily and almost completely digested, while, the crude fiber, pentosans, and other less well-known substances are digested with much more difficulty and less completely. It is, therefore, evidently desirable that starches and sugars should constitute the principal part of the carbohydrates in a feeding stuff, especially in a concentrated feeding stuff. The less valuable carbohydrates, such as pentosans and crude fiber, the presence of which is necessary to give body to the feed, can be supplied by the cheaper coarse fodders. It becomes evident, therefore, that if two concentrated feeds contain the same amounts of protein, fat, and carbohydrates, but in one the carbohydrates consist principally of woody hulls, while in the other they consist principally of starches and sugars, the latter is to be preferred.

DISCUSSION OF RESULTS OF ANALYSES.

Table 1 gives the names of the various cattle foods examined, together with the name and address of the manufacturer. The results of the chemical and microscopical examinations are given in the various tables arranged in groups (cottonseed, linseed, etc.) in connection with the discussion of the data. Where more than one sample of a certain product was examined the individual as well as an average analysis is given. As manufacturers, and in fact the general public, interpret the words bran, middlings, and red-dog flour so differently, the microscopical results of wheat products are not reported under these names, but are recorded as wheat products Nos. 1, 2, and 3. The significance of these numbers and the discussion of the histological features of the various constituents are given under "Microscopical examination," page 74.

TABLE 1.—*Description of samples.*

Serial No.	Name of product.	Name of manufacturer.	Address of manufacturer.
1473	Mixed feed	Thornton & Chester Milling Co.	Buffalo, N. Y.
1474	Dandy corn and oat feed	Commercial Milling Co	Detroit, Mich.
1475	Corn and oat chop	E. L. Potter	Fort Edward, N. Y.
1476	Great Western dairy feed	Great Western Cereal Co	Chicago, Ill.
1477	Boss corn and oat feed	do	Do.
1478	Blue Grass mixed feed	A. Walker & Co	Henderson, Ky.
1479	Flint gluten feed	Flint Mill Co	Milwaukee, Wis.
1480	Oil meal, O. P	The Mann Bros. Co	Buffalo, N. Y.
1481	Dried beet pulp	Alma Sugar Co	Alma, Mich.
1482	Corn meal and oat feed	Mack & Kennedy	Glens Falls, N. Y.
1483	Royal mixed feed	Brooks Elevator Co	Minneapolis, Minn.
1484	Common feed	Lapham & Parks	Glens Falls, N. Y.
1485	Molasses feed	E. P. Mueller	Milwaukee, Wis.
1487	De-Fi corn and oat feed	Elsworth & Co	Buffalo, N. Y.
1488	Puritan ground feed	Paine Bros. Co	Milwaukee, Wis.
1489	Merchants' dairy feed	Merchants' Distilling Co	Terre Haute, Ind.
1492	Ground corn and oats	Barber & Bennett	Albany, N. Y.
1493	Prime cottonseed meal	American Cotton Oil Co	New York City.
1494	Vim oat feed	American Cereal Co	Chicago, Ill.
1495	Hominy chop	W. H. Payne & Sons	231 E. One hundred and twenty-ninth street, New York City.
1496	Arrow corn and oat feed	Oneonta Milling Co	Oneonta, N. Y.
1497	Mixed feed	Rex Mill Co	Kansas City, Mo.
1498	Oil meal, O. P	American Linseed Co	New York City.
1499	X oat feed	American Cereal Co	Chicago, Ill.
1500	Ground feed	W. L. Travis	4 South street, New York City.
1501	Tri-Me mixed feed	Sparks Milling Co	Alton, Ill.
1503	Empire State dairy feed	Clark Bros. & Co	Peoria, Ill.
1504	Excelsior corn and oat feed	Great Western Cereal Co	Chicago, Ill.
1505	Royal oat feed	do	Do.
1506	Blomo feed	Blomo Manufacturing Co	New York City.
1507	Vermont mixed feed	Flint Mill Co	Milwaukee, Wis.
1508	Ground corn and oats	Ogden & Clark	Utica, N. Y.
1509	Stott's honest mixed feed	David Stott	Detroit, Mich.
1510	Corn and oat provender	Oneonta Milling Co	Albany, N. Y.
1511	Ground corn and oats	Browne Bros	Flushing, N. Y.
1512	Linseed oil meal, O. P	Hanenstein & Co	Buffalo, N. Y.
1513	Oil meal, O. P	Hunter Bros	St. Louis, Mo.
1514	Ground feed	H. D. McCord & Son	92-94 Broad street, New York City.
1515	Export brand linseed oil meal, O. P.	Chapin & Co	Buffalo, N. Y.
1516	Corn and oat chop	Knickerbocker Mill & Grain Co.	Albany, N. Y.
1517	Warner's gluten feed	Warner Sugar Refining Co	Chicago, Ill.
1518	Cream oat feed	Great Western Cereal Co	Do.
1519	Green Diamond cottonseed meal.	Chapin & Co	Buffalo, N. Y.
1520	Corn meal and chop feed	George Roberts	Glens Falls, N. Y.
1521	Puritan chick food	Puritan Poultry Farms	Stamford, Conn.
1522	Oil cottonseed meal	F. M. Brodie & Co	Memphis, Tenn.
1523	Creamery feed	Buffalo Cereal Co	Buffalo, N. Y.
1524	Malt sprouts	Oneonta Milling Co	Albany, N. Y.
1525	Mixed feed	The Gardner Mill	Hastings, Minn.
1526	Ground corn and oats	Shaw and Truesdale Co	Second street and Gorwand, Canal, Brooklyn, N. Y.
1527	Dixie cottonseed meal	Humphreys, Godwin & Co	Memphis, Tenn.
1528	Star feed	The Toledo Elevator Co	Toledo, Ohio.
1529	H-O Co.'s poultry food	H-O Co	Buffalo, N. Y.
1530	Brewer's dried grain	E. P. Mueller (jobber)	Milwaukee, Wis.
1531	Hominy feed	American Hominy Co	Indianapolis, Ind.
1532	American poultry food	American Cereal Co	Chicago, Ill.
1533	Buffalo gluten feed	Glucose Sugar Refining Co	Do.
1534	Malt sprouts	E. P. Mueller	Milwaukee, Wis.
1535	Hominy feed	Toledo Elevator Co	Toledo, Ohio.
1536	Ground feed	Fulton Grain and Mill Co	Pacific street, Brooklyn, N. Y.
1537	Ground linseed cake, O. P	A. L. Clements & Co	New York City.
1539	Pioneer barley feed	The Pioneer Cereal Co	Akron, Ohio.
1540	Molasses grains	E. P. Mueller	Milwaukee, Wis.
1541	Creamery feed	Buffalo Cereal Co	Buffalo, N. Y.
1543	Tri-Me mixed feed	Sparks Milling Co	Alton, Ill.
1544	Ground corn and oats	Washburne Supply Co	Pleasantville, N. Y.
1545	Ground feed	J. H. Brett	Mount Vernon, N. Y.
1547	Pekin gluten feed	Illinois Sugar Refining Co	Chicago, Ill.
1548	Ground corn and oats	S. W. Boone	Smith Street, Brooklyn, N. Y.
1549	do	W. H. Paine & Son	231 East One hundred and twenty-ninth street, New York City.
1550	Lenox stock food	Strong Leffert's Co	New York ty.
1551	Common feed	Glens Falls Co	Glens Falls, N. Y.

TABLE 1.—*Description of samples*—Continued.

Serial No.	Name of product.	Name of manufacturer.	Address of manufacturer.
1552	Prime cottonseed meal.........	George B. Robinson, jr. (jobber)	New York City.
1553	Ground linseed cake...........	Milwaukee Linseed Oil Works	Milwaukee, Wis.
1554	Howard's hominy meal........	Buffalo Cereal Co...............	Buffalo, N. Y.
1555	Ground feed.....................	N. Lawrence & Co..............	Dobbs Ferry, N. Y.
1556	Egg builder ration.............	Geo. L. Harding................	Binghamton, N. Y.
1557	Animal meal....................	Bowker Fertilizer Co...........	New York City.
1558	Victor corn and oat feed.......	American Cereal Co............	Chicago, Ill.
1559	Hominy chop...................	Suffern, Hunt & Co............	Decatur, Ill.
1560	Oil meal, O. P..................	Kellogg & Miller...............	Amsterdam, N. Y.
1561	Anchor corn and oat feed......	Illinois Cereal Co...............	Lockport, Ill.
1565	Brewer's dried grain...........	E. P. Mueller...................	Milwaukee, Wis.
1566	Ground corn and oats..........	Thos. Morgan..................	Long Island City, N. Y.
1568	Globe gluten feed...'..........	N. Y. Glucose Co..............	Edgewater, N. J.
1569	Ground feed...................	Brooklyn Elevator and Mill Co.	86 Kent avenue, Brooklyn, N. Y.
1570	....do.....................	J. & L. Adikes.................	Jamaica, N. Y.
1571	....do.....................	Close Bros.....................	Schenectady, N. Y.
1572	Monarch horse feed...........	Oneonta Milling Co............	Albany, N. Y.
1573	Dairy feed....................	Buffalo Cereal Co..............	Buffalo, N. Y.
1574	Schumacker's stock food......	American Cereal Co............	Chicago, Ill.
1575	Blatchford's sugar and flax-seed.	J. W. Barwell..................	Waukegan, Ill.
1576	C. & W. mixed feed...........	Crow & Williams...............	Ossining, N. Y.
1577	Monarch chop feed............	Husted Mill and Elevator Co...	Buffalo, N. Y.
1580	Cottonseed meal..............	H. E. Bridges & Co............	Memphis, Tenn.
1581	Cypher's laying food..........	Cypher's Incubator Co.........	Buffalo, N. Y.
1582	Poultry feed..................	Buffalo Cereal Co..............	Do.
1583	Horse feed.....\..............	.....do.......................	Do.
1584	Mixed feed...................	G. A. Bagley..................	Peekskill, N. Y.
1585	Oil meal, O. P..................	Metzger Seed and Oil Co.......	Toledo, Ohio.
1586	Cow oil meal.................	Union Linseed Co..............	Troy, N. Y.
1587	Niagara corn and oat feed....	Niagara Mill and Elevator Co..	Buffalo, N. Y.
1588	Green oval linseed oil meal....	Flint Mill Co..................	Milwaukee, Wis.
1589	Fourex distillery dried grains..	The J. W. Biles Co.............	Cincinnati, Ohio.
1590	Blatchford's calf meal.........	J. W. Barwell.................	Waukegan, Ill.
1591	Mixed feed (wheat bran, mid-dlings, and flour).	Henry Russell..................	Albany, N. Y.
1596	Star cottonseed meal..........	Sledge & Wells Co.............	Memphis, Tenn.
1597	Snow Flake mixed feed........	Lawrenceburg Roller Mills.....	Lawrenceburg, Ind.
1598	Corn and oat chop............	Buffalo Cereal Co..............	Buffalo, N. Y.
1599	Excelsior corn and oat feed....	Great Western Cereal Co.......	Chicago, Ill.
1601	Malt sprouts..................	Henry Rang & Sons............	Do.
1602	Mixed feed...................	Kehlor Bros...................	St. Louis, Mo.
1603	Capitol corn and oat feed......	Albany City Mills.............	Albany, N. Y.
1604	"O. O." yellow feed...........	Diamond Elevator and Mill Co.	Minneapolis, Minn.
1605	Mixed feed...................	Ogdensburg Roller Mills.......	Ogdensburg, N. Y.
1606	Blue Ribbon distiller's corn grains.	Chas. A. Krause Grain Co......	Milwaukee, Wis.
1607	Monarch ground wheat feed...	F. W. Stock & Son.............	Hillsdale, Mich.
1609	Ground corn, oats, and rye....	Tierney & Dalton..............	Mechanicsville, N. Y.
1610	Molasses feed.................	M. G. Rankin & Co............	Milwaukee, Wis.
1611	Boston feed...................	Imperial Mill Co...............	Duluth, Minn.
1612	Green oval linseed oil meal	Flint Mill Co..................	Milwaukee, Wis.
1613	Model feed...................	J. F. Meyer & Son....'........	Springfield, Mo.
1614	Ajax Flakes..................	Chapin & Co..................	Buffalo, N. Y.
1615	Empire feed..................	Empire Mills..................	Olean, N. Y.
1616	Horse Shoe cottonseed meal...	Hugh Pettit & Co..............	Memphis, Tenn.
1617	Buckeye wheat feed...........	American Cereal Co............	Chicago, Ill.
1618	Indian prime cottonseed meal .	National Cottonseed Product Co.	Memphis, Tenn.
1619	Stott's pure winter wheat mixed feed.	David Stott...................	Detroit, Mich.
1620	Southern Beauty cottonseed meal.	J. G. Falls & Co...............	Memphis, Tenn.
1621	Provender....................	Dixon & Warren...............	Port Byron, N. Y.
1622	Queen gluten feed.............	National Starch Co............	Chicago, Ill.
1623	Mixed feed...................	Webster Mill Co...............	Webster, S. Dak.
1624	Monarch chop feed............	Husted Mill and Elevator Co...	Buffalo, N. Y.
1625	3X corn and oat feed.........	Buffalo Cereal Co..............	Do.
1626	Prime cottonseed meal........	Hayley & Hoskins.............	Memphis, Tenn.
1627	Meal and shorts...............	Clark & Mercer................	Baldwinsville, N. Y.
1628	Germaline....................	Pratt Cereal Oil Co............	Decatur, Ill.
1629	Erie mixed feed...............	Chapin & Co. (jobbers)........	Buffalo, N. Y.
1630	Cottonseed meal..............	Hunter Bros...................	St. Louis, Mo.
1631	Ground oats..................	W. G. Gage & Co..............	Fulton, N. Y.
1693	Scratching food...............	Cypher's Incubator Co.........	Buffalo, N. Y.
1694	Monogram mixed feed.........	H. G. Fertig & Co..............	Minneapolis, Minn.
1695	Fourex XXXX distiller's dried grains.	The J. W. Biles Co.............	Cincinnati, Ohio.
1696	Blood meal...................	The Cudahy Packing Co.......	Kansas City, Kans.
1697	Niagara chop.................	C. E. Allen...................	Niagara Falls, N. Y.
1698	Barley meal..................	Allen V. Smith................	Marcellus Falls, N. Y.
1699	Ground corn and oats.........	Henry Neff....................	Salamanca, N. Y.

TABLE 1.—*Description of samples*—Continued.

Serial No.	Name of product.	Name of manufacturer.	Address of manufacturer.
1700	Star feed	The Toledo Elevator Co	Toledo, Ohio.
1701	Corn and oat chop No. 2	Dayton Milling Co	Tonawanda, N. Y.
1702	Corn and oat chop	S. T. Hoyt	Corning, N. Y.
1703	Buckeye wheat feed	American Cereal Co	Chicago, Ill.
1704	Choice corn and oat provender	Oneonta Milling Co	Oneonta, N. Y.
1705	Royal oat feed	Great Western Cereal Co	Chicago, Ill.
1706	Dixie cottonseed meal	Humphreys, Godwin & Co	Memphis, Tenn.
1708	Export O. P. linseed oil meal	Chapin & Co	Buffalo, N. Y.
1709	Corn and oat chop	Hodgman Milling Co	Painted Post, N. Y.
1710	Niagara corn and oat chop	Niagara Mill and Elevator Co	Buffalo, N. Y.
1711	Unexcelled baby chick food	George L. Harding	Binghamton, N. Y.
1713	Ground corn and oats	The Fall Creek Milling Co	Ithaca, N. Y.
1714	Gluten feed	Peel Bros. Starch Co	Indianapolis, Ind.
1716	Delaware feed	Morris Bros	Oneonta, N. Y.
1717	Sunshine mixed feed	Hunter Bros	St. Louis, Mo.
1718	Prime cottonseed meal	Independent Cotton Oil Co	Memphis, Tenn.
1719	Southern Beauty cottonseed meal.	J. G. Falls & Co	Do.
1720	Globe gluten feed	New York Glucose Co	Edgewater, N. J.
1721	Boston mixed feed	Imperial Milling Co	Duluth, Minn.
1722	Export linseed oil meal, O. P.	Chapin & Co	Buffalo, N. Y.
1723	Schumacker's stock food	American Cereal Co	Chicago, Ill.
1724	Gold Mine mixed feed	The Sheffield Milling Co	Faribault, Minn.
1725	Hominy feed	Suffern, Hunt & Co	Decatur, Ill.
1726	Blatchford's sugar and flaxseed.	J. W. Barwell	Waukegan, Ill.
1727	Malt sprouts	Kane Malting Co	Buffalo, N. Y.
1728	Molasses grains	E. P. Mueller	Milwaukee, Wis.
1729	Lackawanna special horse and cattle feed.	Lackawanna Mill and Elevator Co.	Buffalo, N. Y.
1731	Corn and oat feed	T. R. Peck & Son	Horsehead, N. Y.
1732	Armour's pure blood meal	Armour & Co	Chicago, Ill.
1733	Rye mixed feed	Oneonta Milling Co	Oneonta, N. Y.
1734	Buffalo gluten feed	Glucose Sugar Refining Co	Chicago, Ill.
1735	Malt sprouts	Unknown	Do.
1737	Granulated poultry bone	Armour & Co	Do.
1738	Blatchford's poultry meats	J. W. Barwell	Waukegan, Ill.
1739	Chick food	Cypher's Incubator Co	Buffalo, N. Y.
1740	Niagara corn and oat feed	Niagara Mill and Elevator Co	Do.
1741	X X X corn and oat feed	Buffalo Cereal Co	Do.
1743	King feed	R. P. Moore Milling Co	Princeton, Ind.
1744	Bowker's animal meal	Bowker Fertilizer Co	New York City.
1745	Cottonseed meal	R. W. Biggs & Co	Memphis, Tenn.
1746	Green oval O. P. linseed oil meal.	Flint Mill Co	Milwaukee, Wis.
1748	Coarse poultry bone	Armour & Co	Chicago, Ill.
1750	Old Process oil meal	Spencer Kellog	Buffalo, N. Y.
1752	Golden chop	Victor Mills	Springville, N. Y.
1753	Empire feed	Empire Mills	Olean, N. Y.
1754	Blatchford's calf meal	J. W. Barwell	Waukegan, Ill.
1755	Mixed feed	Bernett, Craft & Kauffman Mill Co.	St. Louis, Mo.
1757	Green Diamond hominy	Chapin & Co	Buffalo, N. Y.
1758	Frumentum hominy feed	U. S. Frumentum Co	Detroit, Mich.
1759	Forcing food	Cypher's Incubator Co	Buffalo, N. Y.
1760	Chop feed	Ellicottville Milling Co	Ellicottville, N. Y.
1761	Hominy feed	Hunter Bros	St. Louis, Mo.
1762	Victor corn and oat feed	American Cereal Co	Chicago, Ill.
1765	Common feed	Nicholas Hotton	Portville, N. Y.
1767	H-O horse feed	The H-O Company	Buffalo, N. Y.
1768	Biles rye (R) grains	The J. W. Biles Co	Cincinnati, Ohio.
1770	Germaline	Pratt Cereal Oil Co	Decatur, Ill.
1771	Warner's gluten feed	Warner Sugar Refining Co	Waukegan, Ill.
1773	Blood meal	Swift & Co	Chicago, Ill.
1774	Winter wheat mixed feed	Commercial Milling Co	Detroit, Mich.
1775	O. P. oil meal	Metzger Seed & Oil Co	Toledo, Ohio.
1776	H-O poultry feed	The H-O Company	Buffalo, N. Y.
1777	Corn and oat chop No. 2	Chase Hibbard Milling Co	Elmira, N. Y.
1779	Mixed feed	Thornton & Chester Milling Co	Buffalo, N. Y.
1780	....do	Blish Milling Co	Seymour, Ind.
1781	Arrow corn and oat feed	Oneonta Milling Co	Oneonta, N. Y.
1782	O. P. linseed meal	Warrenstein & Co	Buffalo, N. Y.
1784	Merchant's high grade dairy feed.	Merchant Distilling Co	Terre Haute, Ind.
1785	Hominy feed	Toledo Elevator Co	Toledo, Ohio.
1786	Chop feed	George Olivir	Olean, N. Y.
1787	Superior mixed feed	Washburne Crosby Co	Minneapolis, Minn.
1788	Prime cottonseed meal	The Hunter Bros. Mill Co	St. Louis, Mo.
1789	Ajax flakes	Chapin & Co	Buffalo, N. Y.

TABLE 1.—*Description of samples*—Continued.

Serial No.	Name of product.	Name of manufacturer.	Address of manufacturer
1790	Linseed oil meal	The Mann Bros	Buffalo, N. Y.
1791	Ground linseed cake, O. P.	Midland Linseed Co	Minneapolis, Minn.
1792	Hominy feed	Buffalo Cereal Co	Buffalo, N. Y.
1793	Vermont mixed feed	Flint Mill Co	Milwaukee, Wis.
1794	Standard Peep O'Day chick food.	The Cornell Incubator Mfg. Co.	Ithaca, N. Y.
1795	Cypher's laying food	Cypher's Incubator Co	Buffalo, N. Y.
1796	O. P. linseed meal	American Linseed Co	New York City.
1797	Export linseed oil meal, O. P.	Chapin & Co	Buffalo, N. Y.
1814	Nursery chick food, No. 1	The Midland Poultry Food Co	Kansas City, Mo.
1815	Growing chick food, No. 2	do	Do.
1817	Boss corn and oat feed	The Great Western Cereal Co	Chicago, Ill.
1818	Provender	C. D. Holbrook	Palmer, Mass.
1819	Union grains—Biles ready ration.	The J. W. Biles Co	Cincinnati, Ohio.
1820	Chick meal	Spratt's Patent Ltd	Newark, N. J.
1821	Malt sprouts	E. P. Mueller	Milwaukee, Wis.
1822	Marsh's pure bone meal	The Geo. E. Marsh Co	Lynn, Mass.
1824	Richmond's horse feed	M. C. Richmond	Adams, Mass.
1825	Mascot mixed feed	Altman	Kempton street, New Bedford, Mass.
1826	Chick feed	Ropes Bros	Salem, Mass.
1827	Crosby's fancy mixed feed	E. Crosby & Co	
1828	Prime cottonseed meal	American Cotton Oil Co	Pine Bluff, Ark.
1829	Dried molasses beet pulp	Alma Sugar Co	Alma, Mich.
1830	Cerealine	Oneonta Milling Co	Oneonta, N. Y.
1831	Haskell's stock food	W. H. Haskell & Co	Toledo, Ohio.
1832	Felker's blended grain	C. H. Felker & Co	Brockton, Mass.
1833	Red Dog. "G"	Bay State Milling Co	Winona, Minn.
1834	Standard middlings	Washburne-Crosby Co	Minneapolis, Minn.
1835	Owl brand pure cottonseed meal.	F. W. Brode & Co	Memphis, Tenn.
1836	Shredded wheat	Thos. W. Emerson Co	Boston, Mass.
1838	Schumacker's oat feed	American Cereal Co	Akron, Ohio.
1839	Prime cottonseed meal	Oliver Refining Co	Portsmouth, Va.
1840	Old Gold brand pure cottonseed meal.	T. H. Burch	Little Rock, Ark.
1841	Fancy middlings	George Fileston Milling Co	St. Cloud, Minn.
1842	Canary brand cottonseed meal.	R. W. Biggs & Co	Memphis, Tenn.
1843	Ajax flakes	Chapin & Co	Buffalo, N. Y.
1844	Bran ⟨H⟩	O. B. Burnham	Beverly, Mass.
1846	O. K. poultry meal	C. H. Felker & Co	Brockton, Mass.
1847	Red Dog ⟨H⟩	Moses Dorr	Boston, Mass.
1848	Buffalo gluten feed	Glucose Sugar Refining Co	Chicago, Ill.
1850	Gold Mine mixed feed	Sheffield King Milling Co	Minneapolis, Minn.
1851	Kidder's hominy feed	F. L. Kidder & Co	Paris, Ill.
1852	Blue Ribbon hominy chop	J. E. Soper & Co	Boston, Mass.
1853	Cottonseed meal	Chapin & Co	St. Louis, Mo.
1854	Cypher's clover meal	Cypher's Incubator Co	Buffalo, N. Y.
1867	Occident mixed feed	Russel-Miller Milling Co	Minneapolis, Minn.
1868	Green Oval Brand O. P. linseed oil meal.	Flint Mill Co	Milwaukee, Wis.
1887	Mixed feed	Straton & Co	Concord, N. H.
1888	Oat middlings	Wm. S. Hill & Co	109 Chamber of Commerce, Boston, Mass.
1889	O. P. oil meal	The Mann Bros. Co	Buffalo, N. Y.
1890	Niagara white meal	Chapin & Co	Boston, Mass.
1891	Chicken feed	Albert Dickinson	Chicago, Ill.
1892	Hominy feed	Unknown	
1893	Cypher's laying food	Cypher's Incubator Co	Buffalo, N. Y.
1894	Middlings	Mystic Milling Co	——, Iowa.
1895	Flour middlings	Washburne-Crosby Co	Minneapolis, Minn.
1896	Prime cottonseed meal	Norton Chapman	Boston, Mass.
1898	Old Gold brand cottonseed meal.	T. H. Burch	Little Rock, Ark.
1899	Old Process oil meal	American Linseed Co	New York City.
1900	Bone meal for cattle	Bowker Fertilizer Co	Boston, Mass.
1901	H & H prime cottonseed meal.	Hayley & Hoskins	Memphis, Tenn.
1902	Hominy feed	Toledo Elevator Co	Toledo, Ohio.
1903	Poultry feed	Poultry Cereal Co	Buffalo, N. Y.
1904	Prime cottonseed meal	American Cotton Oil Co	Brinkley, Ark.
1905	No. 4 c and feather producing food.	The Midland Poultry Co	Kansas City, Mo.
1906	Puritan laying stock food	Puritan Poultry Farms and Mfg. Co.	Stamford, Conn.
1907	Prime cottonseed meal	Oliver Refining Co	Portsmouth, Va.
1908	Cream gluten meal	Illinois Sugar Refining Co	Chicago, Ill.
1909	Sunflower brand prime cottonseed meal.	American Cereal Co	Do.
1910	XXX Cornet Red Dog	Northwestern Consolidated Milling Co.	Minneapolis, Minn.

TABLE 1.—*Description of samples*—Continued.

Serial No.	Name of product.	Name of manufacturer.	Address of manufacturer.
1911	Corn bran, coarse	Glen Mills Cereal Co	Rowley, Mass.
1912	Buffalo gluten feed	Glucose Sugar Refining Co	Chicago, Ill.
1913	Steam-cooked hominy feed	Miner Hillard Milling Co	Miners Mills, Pa.
1914	O. F. oat feed	Wholesaler unknown	
1915	Perfect chick food	W. F. Chamberlain	Kirkwood, Mo.
1917	Adrian Red Dog	Washburne-Crosby Co	Minneapolis, Minn.
1918	Cottonseed meal	J. E. Soper & Co	Boston, Mass.
1919	Golden Bull mixed feed	Lawrenceburg Roller Mills	Lawrenceburg, Ind.
1920	Wyandotte chicken food	Ross Bros	Worcester, Mass.
1921	Phoenix brand prime cotton-seed meal.	D. S. Marshall & Co	Boston, Mass.
1922	XXX corn and oat feed	Buffalo Cereal Co	Buffalo, N. Y.
1923	Scratching feed	Bosworth & Wood	Leominster, Mass.
1924	Malt sprouts	American Malting Co	Syracuse, N. Y.
1925	Blue ribbon distiller's corn grains.	Chas. A. Krause Grain Co	Milwaukee, Wis.
1926	High grade mixed feed	Albans Grain Co	St. Albans, Vt.
1927	Linseed oil meal	American Linseed Oil Co	Chicago, Ill.
1928	Schumacker's stock food	American Cereal Co	Do.
1929	Warner's gluten feed		Waukegan, Ill.
1930	Harding's unexcelled baby chick food.	George L. Harding	Binghamton, N. Y.
1931	Cut green bone	Whitman Rendering Co	Dracut, Mass.
1932	Ground linseed cake	A. L. Clements & Co	New York City.
1933	"OO" yellow feed	Diamond Elevator Milling Co	Minneapolis, Minn.
1934	Oat feed	Albert A. Keene	Chamber of Commerce, Boston, Mass.
1935	Poultry hash	Ropes Bros	Salem, Mass.
1936	High grade scratching feed	H. K. Webster & Co	Lawrence, Mass.
1937	Standard middlings	New Prague Flouring Mill Co	New Prague, Minn.
1938	Flint gluten feed	Flint Mill Co	Milwaukee, Wis.
1940	Choice chicken feed	Moses H. Rolfe	Newburyport, Mass.
1941	Oat feed (F)	W. Wheatley (e)	Manchester, N. H.
1942	Blatchford's sugar and flax-seed.	J. W. Barwell ag nt	Waukegan, Ill.
1944	Webster's scratching feed	H. K. Webster & Co	Lawrence, Mass.
1945	Amsterdam linseed ground cake.	W. N. Potter & Sons	Greenfield, Mass.
1946	O. K. poultry food	Chicopee Rendering Co	Springfield, Mass.
1953	Bran	Blue Earth City Mill Co	Blue Earth City, Minn.
1954	Horse feed	Buffalo Cereal Co	Buffalo, N. Y.
1955	Duchess mixed feed	F. F. Woodward & Co	Ayer, Mass.
1956	Magnolia brand of prime cottonseed meal.	Chas. M. Cox Co	Boston, Mass.
1957	Prime cottonseed meal	Hunter Bros. Milling Co	St. Louis, Mo.
1958	"OO" white feed	Diamond Elevator and Milling Co.	Minneapolis, Minn.
1959	Boston mixed feed	Imperial Milling Co	Duluth, Minn.
1960	Chicken wheat	W. H. Small	Evansville, Ind.
1961	Ogilvie's bran	G. B. Pope & Co	Waltham, Mass.
1962	Vim oat feed	American Cereal Co	Chicago, Ill.
1964	Bran (Holliday)	Moses Dorr	Boston, Mass.
1965	Armour's pure blood meal	Armour & Co	Chicago, Ill.
1968	Cottonseed meal, ABC brand	Augusta Brokerage Co	Augusta, Ga.
1971	Gees ground oil cake compound.	G. E. Grain Co	Minneapolis, Minn.
1972	Creamery feed	Buffalo Cereal Co	Buffalo, N. Y.
1973	Vermont mixed feed	Flint Mill Co	Milwaukee, Wis.
1975	Cream gluten meal	Illinois Sugar Refining Co	Chicago, Ill.
1976	Provender	F. Diehl & Son	Wellesley, Mass.
1977	De-Fi corn and oat feed	Ellsworth & Co	Buffalo, N. Y.
1980	Equality mixed feed	New Prague Flouring Mill Co	New Prague, Minn.
1982	Bran (L) (K)	Wholesaler unknown	
1985	Blue Ribbon distiller's corn grains.	Chas. A. Krause Grain Co	Milwaukee, Wis.
1986	H-O pigeon feed	The H-O Co	Buffalo, N. Y.
1987	Prime cottonseed meal	American Cotton Oil Co	Memphis, Tenn.
1988	Horse feed	The H-O Co	Buffalo, N. Y.
1989	Stott's honest mixed feed	David Stott	Detroit, Mich.
1990	Fourex grains	The J. W. Biles Co	Cincinnati, Ohio.

COTTONSEED MEALS.

The average, maximum, and minimum protein and fat content of various samples of cottonseed meal examined, respectively, in Pennsylvania, New England, and New York are given in the following table:[a]

TABLE 2.—*Percentage of protein and fat in cottonseed meals.*

[Compiled.]

Source of samples.	Number of analyses.	Protein.			Fat.		
		Maximum.	Minimum.	Average.	Maximum.	Minimum.	Average.
Pennsylvania, 1900–1901................	8	46.09	42.50	44.40	12.25	8.77	10.10
New England, 1898–99.................	205	52.60	40.30	45.40	17.00	6.50	11.20
New York, 1898–99.....................	14	50.69	41.68	45.64	13.16	7.56	10.82

The average percentage composition of cottonseed meals reported by Jenkins and Winton[b] is as follows:

Number of analyses...	35
Moisture..	8.2
Ash..	7.2
Protein...	42.3
Crude fiber...	5.6
Fat..	13.1
Nitrogen-free extract	23.6

Taken as a whole, the samples of cottonseed meal examined (Table 3) have a satisfactory protein content. Although most of the samples do not come up to the average found in Pennsylvania, New York, and New England, they approximate the average reported by Jenkins and Winton. Only two samples show such a low protein content as to render them liable to suspicion—namely, Nos. 1745 and 1907. No. 1745 shows a protein content of only about half what it should be. From the large amount of crude fiber and pentosans in the sample, the low fat figure, and the results of the microscopical examination it is evident that an excessive amount of hulls is present in this meal. Sample No. 1907 contains an amount of protein considerably below the average. The other figures for this sample, however, are not especially suspicious, and, since another sample of the same goods has an average protein content, it is probable that it is not adulterated in any way.

The figures for crude fiber are suspiciously large in only four cases—namely, Nos. 1552, 1630, 1788, 1745. Since in sample 1552 the determinations other than crude fiber compare fairly well with the average, it is probable that this rather high crude fiber has no significance.

[a] Report of the Pennsylvania State College for 1900–1901, under report of chemist.
[b] U. S. Dept. Agr., Office of Experiment Stations, Bul. No. 11, A Compilation of Analyses of American Feeding Stuffs.

In samples Nos. 1630 and 1788 not only do the crude fiber figures show a slight tendency to be above the average, but this is also true of the pentosan figures. At the same time the protein and fat figures for these samples, without being markedly low, show a tendency to be below normal. In No. 1788 an excess of cotton fiber was found microscopically. It would, therefore, appear that these two samples contained a somewhat larger amount than normal of hulls or cotton fiber. It is only fair to add that a third sample of the same goods as samples Nos. 1630 and 1788 had a good average composition. Sample No. 1745 was discussed in the preceding paragraph.

The figures for pentosans are suspiciously large in only three cases, which have already been discussed.

Most of the samples examined show the presence of a very small amount of starch. It is probable, however, that no starch was really present, the small amount reported being due to inherent errors in the method of analysis.

For the sake of uniformity of expression the non-reducing sugars are reported as sucrose. They are probably present, however, almost entirely in the form of raffinose, as shown by Scheibler and Mittelmeiers,[a] Berthelot,[b] Withers and Fraps,[c] and others. None varies so much from the general average as to appear suspicious, except in the case of sample No. 1745, which has already been discussed. Most of the samples contained no reducing sugars, while a few contained a very small amount.

As a whole, the figures for crude fat are below the various averages shown by the compiled data. It would appear from this that the fat is now more completely removed from the seeds than in the past. Only two fats are so low as to appear suspicious—namely, Nos. 1788 and 1745. A discussion of both of these samples has already been given.

---

[a] Ber. d. chem. Ges., 1889, *22*: 3118.

[b] Compt. rend., 1886, *103*: 533.

[c] North Carolina Agr. Exper. Stat., Bul. No. 179.

TABLE 3.—*Cottonseed meals (percentage composition).*

Serial No.	Name and brand.	Moisture.	Calculated to basis of original sample.									Calculated to a moisture-free basis.									Raw materials identified by microscopical examination.
			Ash.	Crude protein.	Crude fiber.	Pentosan.	Starch.	Sucrose.	Reducing sugars.	Ether extract.	Undetermined.	Ash.	Crude protein.	Crude fiber.	Pentosan.	Starch.	Sucrose.	Reducing sugars.	Ether extract.	Undetermined.	
1493	Cottonseed meal, prime	7.50	7.72	42.63	8.73	8.03	0.48	4.56	0.24	10.33	9.78	8.35	46.09	9.44	8.68	0.52	4.93	0.26	11.16	10.57	Cottonseed meal.
1828	....do........	7.44	6.68	39.70	5.63	8.42	0	6.06	0	9.10	16.97	7.22	42.89	6.08	9.09	0	6.54	0	9.84	18.33	Do.
1904	....do........	6.44	7.82	43.36	5.98	8.45	0	6.13	0	10.10	11.72	8.36	46.34	6.39	9.03	0	6.55	0	10.80	12.53	Do.
1987	....do........	8.36	6.69	41.19	7.73	9.47	.62	5.68	0	8.37	11.89	7.30	44.95	8.43	10.34	.67	6.19	0	9.14	12.98	Do.
	Average........	7.44	7.23	41.72	7.02	8.59	.27	5.61	.06	9.47	12.59	7.81	45.07	7.58	9.28	.30	6.05	.06	10.24	13.60	
59	seed meal, Green Diamond.	6.74	7.25	45.75	5.06	7.62	.19	5.52	.26	9.35	12.22	7.77	49.07	5.42	8.21	.20	5.92	.28	10.03	13.10	Do.
132	Cottonseed meal, oil....	5.99	6.96	46.13	5.13	7.56	.62	8.20	.26	9.05	10.10	7.35	49.08	5.45	8.04	.69	8.72	.28	9.63	10.76	Do.
137	seed meal, Dixie.	7.36	7.40	44.38	5.67	7.89	.19	6.38	.29	8.75	11.69	7.99	47.89	6.12	8.52	.20	6.90	.31	9.45	12.62	Do.
1706	....do........	4.24	7.83	44.81	7.29	8.70	.20	5.87	0	7.87	13.19	8.18	46.79	7.61	9.09	.21	6.13	0	8.22	13.77	Do.
	Average........	5.80	7.61	44.59	6.48	8.29	.20	6.13	.15	8.31	12.44	8.09	47.34	6.82	8.81	.21	6.52	.16	8.84	13.21	
1552	Cottonseed meal, prime	7.05	6.14	40.50	9.98	9.67	.83	5.38	.23	10 00	10.22	6.61	43.56	10.74	10.40	.89	5.79	.25	10.76	11.00	Do.
1580	seed meal....	6.01	6.98	43.81	7.11	8.40	1.85	6.33	.15	9.10	9.68	7.43	46.61	7.56	8.94	1.97	6.73	.16	10.30	10.30	Do.
1596	seed meal, Star..	6.49	6.41	45.38	6.70	8.14	.65	6.39	.27	8.23	11.34	6.85	48.56	7.16	8.70	.69	6.83	.29	8.80	12.12	Do.
1616	Cottonseed meal, Horseshoe.	7.30	6.60	42.44	7.16	8.53	.90	6.25	.16	10.15	10.51	7.12	45.80	7.72	9.20	.97	6.74	.17	10.95	11.33	Do.
1618	seed meal, Indian Prime.	6.13	6.82	46.44	4.68	7.15	.25	6.78	.22	10.28	11.25	7.27	49.47	4.99	7.62	.26	7.22	.23	10.95	11.99	Do.
1620	Cottonseed meal, Southern Beauty.	7.62	8.01	43.63	5.46	7.29	0	6.41	.19	10.32	11.07	8.67	47.24	5.91	7.89	0	6.94	.20	11.18	11.98	Do.
1719	....do........	6.50	7.06	40.88	6.61	8.85	.48	6.82	0	11.24	11.56	7.55	43.74	7.07	9.46	.51	7.29	0	12.02	12.36	Do.
	Average........	7.06	7.53	42.26	6.03	8.07	.24	6.62	.09	10.78	11.32	8.11	45.49	6.49	8.68	.25	7.11	.10	11.60	12.17	
1626	Cottonseed meal, prime	7.26	7.08	42.19	6.42	8.57	1.51	5.95	0	10.21	10.81	7.62	45.40	6.91	9.42	1.63	6.40	0	10.99	11.63	Do.
1901	....do........	8.48	7.67	44.91	7.79	6.38	0	4.59	0	9.73	10.45	8.38	49.08	8.51	6.97	0	5.01	0	10.63	11.41	Do.
	Average........	7.87	7.38	43.55	7.10	7.48	.75	5.27	0	9.97	10.63	8.00	47.24	7.71	8.20	.82	5.70	0	10.81	11.52	
1630	seed meal, prime	6.94	6.67	39.81	10.36	9.92	.65	6.10	0	8.52	11.03	7.17	42.77	11.13	10.66	.70	6.56	0	9.16	11.85	Do.
1788	....do........	7.96	6.43	40.00	9.58	10.20	.22	6.01	0	6.72	12.88	6.99	43.46	10.41	11.08	.24	6.53	0	7.30	13.99	Cottonseed meal; considerable cotton fiber.

No.	Description																			Cottonseed meal.
1957	......do......	7.26	7.82	40.94	5.47	8.19	0	5.78	0	10.32	14.22	8.43	44.16	5.90	8.83	0	6.23	0	11.12	15.33	Cottonseed meal.
	Average.........	7.38	6.97	40.25	8.47	9.44	.29	5.96	0	8.51	12.71	7.53	43.46	9.15	10.19	.31	6.44	0	9.19	13.73	Do.
1718	Cottonseed meal, prime, Owl Brand.	6.69	7.37	42.94	5.63	7.67	.75	6.29	0	9.63	11.03	7.90	46.03	6.03	8.22	.80	6.74	0	10.32	13.96	Cottonseed meal; large amount of seed coats.
1745	Cottonseed meal......	8.11	4.80	22.38	20.26	23.16	.40	3.06	0	4.93	12.81	5.22	24.37	22.05	25.20	.53	3.33	0	5.36	13.94	Cottonseed meal.
1835	Pure cottonseed meal.	11.43	7.46	43.86	8.73	6.81	0	5.80	0	9.18	6.73	8.42	49.53	9.86	7.68	0	6.55	0	10.36	7.61	Cottonseed meal.
1839	Cottonseed meal, prime	9.54	6.36	42.05	6.09	8.67	0	6.54	0	8.73	12.02	7.04	46.48	6.73	9.59	0	7.23	0	9.65	13.28	Do.
1907	......do......	8.90	6.34	37.90	9.06	5.84	.34	8.71	0	7.99	14.92	6.95	41.61	9.95	6.41	.37	9.56	0	8.77	16.38	Do.
	Average.........	9.22	6.35	39.98	7.57	7.25	.17	7.63	0	8.36	13.47	7.00	44.04	8.34	8.00	.19	8.39	0	9.21	14.83	Do.
1840	Pure cottonseed meal, Old Gold.	7.45	6.96	43.91	5.95	8.40	.29	5.95	0	8.79	12.30	7.52	47.45	6.43	9.07	.32	6.43	0	9.49	13.29	Do.
1898	......do......	8.30	6.88	42.16	6.55	8.17	0	5.90	0	9.55	12.49	7.50	45.98	7.14	8.91	0	6.43	0	10.42	13.62	Do.
	Average.........	7.88	6.92	43.03	6.25	8.29	.15	5.92	0	9.17	12.39	7.51	46.71	6.78	8.99	.16	6.43	0	9.96	13.46	Do.
1842	Cottonseed meal, Canary.	12.96	7.04	41.04	6.81	7.22	0	5.59	0	7.40	11.94	8.09	47.14	7.82	8.31	0	6.42	0	8.50	13.72	Do.
1853	Cottonseed meal......	9.39	7.73	44.86	4.71	6.62	0	5.78	0	8.79	12.12	8.53	49.50	5.20	7.31	0	6.39	0	9.70	13.37	Do.
1896	Cottonseed meal, prime.	8.80	6.31	40.78	6.71	9.16	0	6.04	0	8.86	13.34	6.92	44.73	7.35	10.04	0	6.62	0	9.71	14.63	Do.
1909	Cottonseed meal, Prime Sunflower.	7.36	4.37	44.34	6.58	8.06	.24	6.07	0	8.50	14.48	4.72	47.86	7.10	8.70	.26	6.55	0	9.18	15.63	Do.
1918	Cottonseed meal......	9.34	6.50	41.72	6.45	8.51	0	5.44	0	9.17	12.87	7.17	46.01	7.12	9.39	0	6.00	0	10.12	14.19	Do.
1921	Cottonseed meal, Prime Phenix.	9.57	7.53	41.19	6.85	9.02	0	5.87	0	9.43	10.54	8.32	45.55	7.58	9.97	0	6.49	0	10.43	11.66	Do.
1956	Cottonseed meal, Magth.	8.27	7.10	43.24	6.40	8.45	0	5.98	0	9.92	10.64	7.74	47.14	6.98	9.21	0	6.52	0	10.81	11.60	Do.
1968	...eed meal, ABC.	8.04	7.07	43.73	6.80	8.56	0	5.88	0	8.65	11.27	7.69	47.55	7.39	9.31	0	6.40	0	9.40	12.26	Do.

LINSEED MEALS.

The average, maximum, and minimum protein and fat content of various samples of linseed meal examined in Pennsylvania, New England, and New York are given in the following table:[a]

TABLE 4.—*Percentage of protein and fat in linseed meals.*

[Compiled.]

Source of sample.	Number of analyses.	Protein.			Fat.		
		Maximum.	Minimum.	Average.	Maximum.	Minimum.	Average.
"Old process" meal:							
Pennsylania, 1900–1901.............	24	37.81	29.69	34.10	8.88	3.54	6.04
New England, 1898–99..............	25	38.90	31.80	35.70	9.60	2.70	7.20
New York, 1898–99.................	14	38.19	28.69	35.74	8.86	5.72	7.19
"New process" meal:							
Pennsylvania, 1900–1901...........	3	34.63	34.00	34.25	2.92	2.19	2.63
New England, 1898–99..............	31	42.20	39.60	38.20	3.50	1.80	2.40
New York, 1898–99.................	5	37.56	35.19	36.14	4.79	2.91	3.57

The average composition of linseed meals reported by Jenkins and Winton[b] is as follows:

TABLE 5.—*Average percentage composition of linseed meals.*

[Compiled.]

Kind of meal.	Number of analyses.	Moisture.	Ash.	Protein.	Crude fiber.	Nitrogen-free extract.	Fat.
"Old process" meals..............	21	9.20	5.7	32.9	8.9	35.4	7.9
"New process" meals.............	14	10.10	5.8	33.2	9.5	38.4	3.0

Taken as a whole the crude protein content of the samples of linseed meal examined is satisfactory (Table 6). A considerable number of the samples do not come up to any of the above averages, but they are, in the majority of cases, not sufficiently below the general average to excite any suspicion of adulteration. The only samples sold under the name of linseed meal that excite any suspicion at all (because of their low protein content) are Nos. 1537, 1868, and 1791. Sample No. 1537 not only contains a slightly low amount of protein, but shows an amount of crude fiber several per cent higher than the average and a larger amount of reducing sugars than other samples. The microscopical examination explains this matter by showing the presence of a wheat product mixed with the linseed meal. The composition of another sample of this product is satisfactory, although a small amount of some leguminous plant is shown to be present. Sample No. 1868 contains a slightly low

[a] Report of Pennsylvania State College for 1900–1901, report of chemist.
[b] U. S. Dept. Agr., Office of Experiment Stations, Bul. No. 11, A Compilation of Analyses of American Feeding Stuffs.

amount of protein, but this has no significance when it is noted that other samples of the same product have a satisfactory composition. Sample No. 1791 also has a somewhat low protein content; since, however, all other determinations on this sample are above suspicion, no significance is to be attached to the low protein content.

Because of the name and microscopical examination, sample No. 1971 was classed under linseed meals, although its low protein and high starch content show that it is not straight linseed meal. The microscopic examination shows the presence of a wheat product.

A considerable number of the samples examined contain a smaller percentage of fat than is given in any of the compiled averages, but they are not so much below the averages as to excite suspicion, except in two cases, namely, Nos. 1927 and 1797. Sample No. 1927 would appear from the fat figures to be made according to the new process. No. 1797 contains considerably less fat than the average linseed meal. Since, however, three other samples of the same goods contain a satisfactory amount of fat, it is probable that the low fat content in this single sample has no significance.

The microscopical examination of this group of samples shows that the majority of them contain weed seeds in greater or less abundance. Small amounts of the various weed seeds are to be expected, and it is only when they are of a poisonous variety or in excessive quantities that their presence is reprehensible.

TABLE 6.—Linseed oil meal (percentage composition).

Serial No.	Name and brand.	Moisture.	Calculated to basis of original sample.									Calculated to a moisture-free basis.									Raw materials identified by microscopic examination.
			Ash.	Crude protein.	Crude fiber.	Pentosan.	Starch.	Sucrose.	Reducing sugars.	Ether extract.	Undetermined.	Ash.	Crude protein.	Crude fiber.	Pentosan.	Starch.	Sucrose.	Reducing sugars.	Ether extract.	Undetermined.	
1480a	Linseed oil meal, O. P.	8.87	4.72	35.75	8.23	11.26	4.46	1.92	0	8.66	16.13	5.18	39.23	9.03	12.36	4.89	2.09	0	9.50	17.72	Linseed oil meal, smartweed seed.
1700a	....do.........	8.97	4.86	35.56	8.62	12.19	4.76	2.36	0	7.91	14.77	5.34	39.07	9.47	13.39	5.23	2.59	0	8.69	16.22	Linseed oil meal.
1889a	....do.........	11.69	4.68	34.50	6.94	11.21	7.30	2.28	0	6.06	15.34	5.30	39.08	7.86	12.68	8.27	2.58	0	6.86	17.37	Linseed oil meal, seed.
	Average.....	9.84	4.75	35.27	7.93	11.55	5.51	2.19	0	7.54	15.42	5.27	39.13	8.79	12.81	6.13	2.43	0	8.35	17.10	
1498	Linseed oil meal, O. P.	8.89	4.92	32.63	8.43	10.91	2.85	2.45	0	7.39	21.53	5.40	35.82	9.25	11.97	3.13	2.69	0	8.11	23.63	Linseed meal, pigweed, rough pigweed, smartweed, charlock, seed.
1796	....do.........	8.93	4.78	36.13	8.06	11.74	4.97	2.12	0	7.30	15.97	5.25	39.68	8.85	12.89	5.46	2.33	0	8.01	17.53	Linseed meal, seed.
1899	....do.........	10.88	5.18	32.55	8.30	11.56	7.31	2.59	0	7.10	14.53	5.81	36.54	9.32	12.98	8.17	2.91	0	7.97	16.30	Linseed meal.
	Average.....	9.57	4.96	33.77	8.26	11.40	5.04	2.39	0	7.26	17.34	5.49	37.35	9.14	12.61	5.59	2.64	0	8.03	19.15	
1927	Linseed oil meal, O. P.	11.70	6.46	36.78	8.67	11.30	4.72	2.16	0	2.34	15.87	7.31	41.66	9.81	12.81	5.35	2.57	0	2.52	17.97	Linseed meal.
1515b	Linseed oil meal, O. P. Export.	8.60	5.39	30.00	7.89	10.18	3.47	2.52	0	6.78	20.17	5.90	32.83	8.63	11.13	9.27	2.76	0	7.42	22.06	Linseed meal, pigweed, smartweed.
1708b	....do.........	5.23	5.13	30.56	9.46	13.10	4.69	1.82	0	6.19	23.82	5.41	32.25	9.98	13.83	4.95	1.92	0	6.53	25.13	Linseed meal, pigweed, rough pigweed.
1722b	....do.........	8.75	5.24	31.88	8.55	7.14	6.19	2.52	0	7.55	22.18	5.74	34.96	9.37	7.82	6.78	2.76	0	8.27	24.30	Linseed meal, smartweed, pigweed, Brassica (sp.).
1797b	....do.........	8.56	6.39	30.50	6.80	10.79	9.93	2.26	0	4.75	18.02	6.99	33.36	9.62	11.80	10.86	2.47	0	5.19	19.71	Linseed meal, pigweed, Brassica sp.
	Average.....	7.78	5.54	30.73	8.67	10.30	7.32	2.28	0	6.32	21.05	6.01	33.35	9.40	11.15	7.96	2.48	0	6.85	22.80	
1537	Ground linseed cake, O. P.	7.98	4.80	29.75	12.68	11.62	6.45	2.48	0.59	6.05	17.60	5.22	32.35	13.78	12.63	7.01	2.70	0.61	6.57	19.13	Linseed meal, charlock and W. P. No. 2.
1932	....do.........	8.73	5.77	31.16	9.34	10.89	4.39	2.58	0	5.31	21.83	6.32	34.15	10.23	11.93	4.81	2.82	0	5.82	23.92	Linseed meal, some legume, race of pigweed seed.
	Average.....	8.36	5.28	30.46	11.01	11.25	5.42	2.53	0.29	5.68	19.72	5.77	33.25	12.01	12.28	5.91	2.76	0.30	6.20	21.52	
1585	Linseed oil meal, O. P.	7.78	5.02	33.25	8.67	10.37	8.47	2.20	0	6.40	17.84	5.44	36.06	9.40	11.24	9.18	2.39	0	6.94	19.34	Linseed meal, pigweed (rough), smartweed.

No.	Description	8.14	5.71	33.25	8.69	11.38	7.59	2.46	0	6.48	16.30	6.21	36.21	9.46
1775	...do...	8.14	5.71	33.25	8.69	11.38	7.59	2.46	0	6.48	16.30	6.21	36.21	9.46
	Average...	7.96	5.37	33.25	8.68	10.87	8.03	2.33	0	6.44	17.07	5.82	36.14	9.43
1588	Linseed oil meal, Green Oval.	7.20	5.40	33.63	7.85	11.33	6.85	2.87	0	5.08	19.79	5.82	36.24	8.46
1612	...do...	9.63	5.87	30.13	9.58	10.47	10.08	1.88	0	5.19	17.17	6.50	33.35	10.60
1746	...do...	8.28	6.49	32.44	8.54	10.99	4.59	2.52	0	5.76	20.39	7.07	35.38	9.31
1868	...do...	11.38	6.28	29.63	8.99	11.25	6.46	2.56	0	5.76	17.69	7.09	33.46	10.14
	Average...	9.12	6.01	31.46	8.74	11.01	6.99	2.46	0	5.45	18.76	6.62	34.61	9.63
1512	Linseed oil meal, O.P.	8.83	4.77	35.69	7.08	10.79	4.50	2.56	0	6.71	18.47	5.23	39.15	8.42
1513	...do...	8.74	4.99	32.81	8.86	10.91	6.97	2.36	0	5.65	18.71	5.47	35.95	9.71
1553	Ground linseed cake.	7.49	5.44	33.13	8.52	10.28	6.22	2.50	0	8.28	18.14	5.88	35.82	9.21
1560	Linseed oil meal, O.P.	8.44	4.89	35.25	7.38	11.53	5.25	2.40	0	8.38	16.48	5.34	38.51	8.06
1586c	Linseed oil meal, Cow.	8.24	4.76	34.56	8.21	10.68	4.55	3.09	0	5.27	20.64	5.19	37.66	8.95
1750	Linseed oil meal, O.P.	7.75	4.68	33.31	7.82	10.80	6.47	2.64	0	12.98	13.55	5.07	36.11	8.48
1782	...do...	8.11	4.91	36.44	7.55	11.74	4.78	2.26	0	6.76	17.45	5.34	39.67	8.22
1791a	...do...	8.74	4.84	29.31	8.50	10.50	12.65	2.47	0	8.25	14.74	5.30	32.13	9.31
1945	Linseed ground cake, Amsterdam.	12.37	4.41	32.55	7.34	10.79	3.32	2.32	0	5.67	21.23	5.03	37.16	8.38
1971	Gee's ground oil cake compound.	13.02	4.35	14.54	9.45	8.26	24.98	2.79	0	5.06	17.55	5.00	16.72	10.87

a See page 67.   b See page 64.

CORN PRODUCTS.

The average composition of the two types of corn, dent and flint, and of Indian corn-meal and gluten-meal, as given by Jenkins and Winton,[a] is as follows:

TABLE 7.—*Average percentage composition of corn, corn-meal, and gluten-meal.*

[Compiled.]

Material.	Number of analyses.	Mois-ture.	Ash.	Protein.	Crude fiber.	Nitro-gen-free extract.	Fat.
Whole corn, dent..................	86	10. 6	1. 5	10. 3	2. 2	70. 4	5. 0
Whole corn, flint..................	68	11. 3	1. 4	10. 5	1. 7	70. 1	5. 0
Corn-meal.........................	77	15. 0	1. 4	9. 2	1. 9	68. 7	3. 8
Gluten-meal.......................	32	9. 6	. 7	29. 4	1. 6	52. 4	6. 3

The average, maximum, and minimum protein and fat content of gluten feeds examined in Pennsylvania, New York, and New England [a] from 1898 to 1901 is as follows:

TABLE 8.—*Percentage of protein and fat in gluten feeds.*

[Compiled.]

Description of sample.	Number of analyses.	Protein.			Fat.		
		Max-imum.	Min-imum.	Average.	Max-imum.	Min-imum.	Average.
Pennsylvania, 1900–1901:							
All analyses.....................	11	27. 00	24. 00	25. 71	3. 55	2. 19	2. 64
Glucose Sugar Refining Co.'s brands.........................	7	26. 75	24. 00	25. 58	3. 53	2. 19	2. 81
New England, 1898–99:							
Buffalo gluten-feed...............	34	29. 60	25. 30	27. 50	4. 70	2. 30	3.10
Diamond gluten-feed.............	30	30. 10	20. 30	23. 60	4. 00	2. 00	3. 00
New York:							
Buffalo gluten-feed, 1899..........	6	27. 63	21. 31	26. 10	4. 67	3. 38	3. 71
Diamond gluten-feed, 1899........	2	20. 56	20. 00	20. 28	5. 21	3. 40	4. 30
All analyses, 1900.................	21	....	....	23. 75	....	....	4. 55
Buffalo gluten-feed, 1900..........	3	27. 00	24. 10	25. 90	5. 00	2. 90	3. 90
Diamond gluten-feed, 1900........	3	25. 90	24. 40	25. 30	3. 60	2. 80	3. 20

The protein content, and in fact the entire composition, of the various samples reported in Table 10 under the name gluten feed is satisfactory. While samples Nos. 1479 and 1938 are somewhat lower in their protein content than the other samples examined, there is no evidence of adulteration. A number of the samples have a fat content considerably lower than the averages given in Table 8, but this fact does not have any especial significance, since gluten feeds are sold for their nitrogen rather than their fat content. The two samples of gluten-meal examined show a very satisfactory protein content.

---

[a] Loc. cit.

Samples Nos. 1535, 1785, and 1902 are all somewhat below the average in fat and above the average in crude fiber, and the last two are slightly below the average in protein. This tendency is not sufficiently marked to indicate adulteration, but would seem to show the presence of more hulls than are found in the average sample. No. 1757 gives practically the same results as the samples just mentioned.

All of the samples examined, except two or three, show somewhat low figures for fat, although not low enough in any case to give rise to suspicion of intentional adulteration.

a Loc. cit.
b Report of the Connecticut Agricultural Experiment Station for 1905, Part III.

TABLE 10.—*Corn products (percentage composition).*

Serial No.	Name and brand.	Moisture.	Original: Ash.	Crude protein.	Crude fiber.	Pentosan.	Starch.	Sucrose.	Reducing sugars.	Ether extract.	Undetermined.	MF: Ash.	Crude protein.	Crude fiber.	Pentosan.	Starch.	Sucrose.	Reducing sugars.	Ether extract.	Undetermined.	Raw materials identified by microscopical examination.
1479	Gluten feed, Flint...	8.08	1.00	22.94	7.23	16.93	31.31	0	0	1.73	10.78	1.09	24.95	7.87	18.42	34.06	0	0	1.88	11.73	Corn hulls and germs, and cooked starch, probably glucose factory by-product.
1938	...do...	9.73	1.04	21.36	9.38	15.54	31.82	0.25	0	1.92	8.96	1.15	23.66	10.39	17.21	35.26	0.28	0	2.13	9.92	Do.
	Average...	8.90	1.02	22.15	8.30	16.24	31.57	.12	0	1.83	9.87	1.12	24.30	9.13	17.81	34.66	.14	0	2.02	10.82	
1517	Gluten feed, Warner's	7.74	.81	24.38	7.72	17.40	32.15	0	0	1.77	8.03	.89	26.42	8.37	18.86	34.84	0	0	1.92	8.70	Do.
1771	...do...	8.09	1.23	25.63	8.06	18.74	29.25	.15	.50	2.91	5.44	1.34	27.88	8.77	20.37	31.82	.16	.54	3.18	5.91	Do.
1929	...do...	9.15	1.45	24.42	8.41	17.36	28.38	0	.58	2.26	7.99	1.59	26.88	9.25	19.10	31.26	0	.64	2.49	8.79	Do.
	Average...	8.33	1.16	24.81	8.06	17.83	29.93	.05	.36	2.31	7.16	1.27	27.06	8.80	19.45	32.64	.05	.40	2.53	7.80	
1533	Gluten feed, Buffalo.	7.24	2.51	23.81	7.27	15.22	32.15	.37	1.41	3.07	6.95	2.71	25.67	7.84	16.41	34.66	.42	1.52	3.31	7.49	Do.
1734	...do...	7.59	2.84	24.50	7.27	14.94	28.03	.54	2.33	3.17	8.79	3.07	26.51	7.87	16.17	36.17	.58	2.52	3.43	9.51	Do.
1848	...do...	6.67	.92	24.22	7.62	17.93	32.87	0	.28	2.17	7.32	.98	25.95	8.16	19.21	35.23	0	.29	2.33	7.85	Do.
1912	...do...	9.75	1.92	24.44	7.05	16.27	28.32	0	.70	1.85	9.70	2.13	27.08	7.81	18.02	31.39	0	.77	2.05	10.75	
	Average...	7.81	2.05	24.24	7.30	16.09	30.35	.23	1.18	2.56	8.19	2.22	26.30	7.92	17.45	32.91	.25	1.27	2.78	8.90	
1568	Gluten Globe	7.22	1.65	25.31	8.25	16.74	28.08	.34	0	1.86	10.55	1.78	27.30	8.89	18.04	30.26	.36	.38	2.00	11.37	Do.
1720	...do...	7.68	1.70	28.50	7.76	16.62	24.09	.08	.35	2.95	10.27	1.84	30.90	8.40	18.00	26.09	.08	0	3.19	11.12	Do.
	Average...	7.45	1.68	26.91	8.01	16.68	26.08	.21	.17	2.40	10.41	1.81	29.10	8.65	18.02	28.18	.22	.19	2.59	11.24	
1547	Gluten feed, Pekin.	7.17	2.13	27.56	7.21	15.63	28.35	.08	.68	2.39	8.80	2.29	29.70	7.77	16.84	30.53	.09	.73	2.57	9.48	Do.
1622	Gluten feed, Queen.	9.17	1.09	24.06	9.26	21.01	26.64	0	0	1.41	7.36	1.20	28.49	10.19	23.13	29.34	0	0	1.55	8.10	Do.
1714	...do feed	7.05	.73	27.19	3.88	8.13	44.42	0	0	1.39	7.21	.78	29.26	4.17	8.75	47.83	0	0	1.50	7.71	Do.
1908	Gluten Cream.	9.25	1.16	43.13	2.04	10.08	30.78	0	.60	.45	2.51	1.28	47.53	2.25	11.10	33.92	0	.66	.48	2.78	Do.
1975	...do...	11.73	1.48	39.82	1.84	6.04	34.33	0	0	1.29	3.47	1.67	45.13	2.08	6.84	38.90	0	0	1.46	3.93	Do.
	Average...	10.49	1.32	41.47	1.94	8.06	32.56	0	.30	.87	2.99	1.48	46.33	2.16	8.97	36.41	0	.33	.97	3.35	
1911	Corn bran...	12.02	1.53	8.50	10.37	26.07	27.29	.13	.29	2.78	11.02	1.74	9.66	11.79	29.64	31.01	.15	.33	3.16	12.52	Coarse corn hulls.

No.	Name																				Remarks
1628	Germaline	8.93	4.25	12.75	4.05	9.94	51.60	4.98	1.65	1.33	.52	4.67	14.00	4.45	10.91	56.66	5.47	1.81	1.46	.57	A corn product, probably corn meal with some excess of hulls and germs.
1770	....do....	8.68	3.82	12.19	4.41	11.84	45.09	5.34	1.66	1.42	5.55	4.18	13.35	4.83	12.96	49.38	5.85	1.82	1.55	6.08	Do.
	Average	8.82	4.03	12.47	4.23	10.89	48.35	5.16	1.65	1.37	3.03	4.42	13.68	4.64	11.94	53.02	5.66	1.82	1.50	3.32	
1830	Cerealine	8.81	4.28	12.48	4.30	9.24	47.61	3.41	.39	1.54	7.94	4.09	13.68	4.71	10.14	52.21	3.74	.43	1.69	8.71	Corn product.
1890	Niagara white meal	12.72	5.09	9.30	2.49	7.01	52.76	1.64	.37	3.04	4.98	5.83	10.65	2.85	8.03	60.46	1.88	.43	4.17	5.70	Corn-meal.
1535	Hominy feed	8.04	2.92	9.56	6.74	13.30	49.84	2.86	.24	5.99	.51	3.18	10.40	7.33	14.46	54.20	3.11	.26	6.51	.55	Corn product, consisting of hulls, endosperm, and germ.
1785	....do....	8.65	2.33	8.94	5.78	10.92	48.59	1.55	.08	5.59	6.97	2.56	9.79	6.33	11.95	53.18	1.70	.74	6.12	7.63	Do.
1902	....do....	11.92	2.92	8.61	6.40	9.60	46.52	1.57	.93	4.89	6.64	3.32	9.78	7.27	10.90	52.81	1.79	1.05	5.55	7.53	Do.
	Average	9.54	2.72	9.04	6.31	11.27	48.32	1.99	.62	5.49	4.70	3.02	9.99	6.98	12.44	53.40	2.20	.68	6.06	5.23	Corn-meal, consisting of hulls, endosperm and germ.
1559	Hominy chop	8.99	2.40	10.00	4.76	11.95	52.56	1.89	.43	6.22	.80	2.64	10.99	5.23	13.13	57.75	2.08	.47	6.83	.88	Do.
1725	....do....	8.66	2.59	10.06	4.39	10.65	48.92	2.56	.58	6.74	4.85	2.88	11.01	4.81	11.66	53.57	2.80	.63	7.38	5.31	Do.
	Average	8.83	2.49	10.03	4.58	11.30	50.74	2.22	.50	6.48	2.83	2.73	11.00	5.02	12.40	55.66	2.44	.55	7.11	3.09	Do.
832d	Hominy chop, Blue Bell.	11.29	2.34	9.96	3.54	9.01	48.35	1.83	.56	6.66	6.46	2.63	11.23	3.98	10.16	54.53	2.06	.63	7.50	7.28	Do.
1495	Hominy ch.	9.31	2.43	10.13	3.57	9.06	49.78	1.90	.82	6.99	6.01	2.68	11.17	3.94	9.99	54.89	2.09	.90	7.71	6.63	Do.
1531	Hominy feed	7.76	3.10	10.81	3.84	10.35	51.46	2.56	.23	9.38	.51	3.36	11.72	4.16	11.22	55.81	2.77	.25	10.16	.55	Do.
1554	Hominy meal, Howard's.	8.77	2.75	9.94	3.73	8.83	52.31	2.86	.17	7.89	2.71	3.01	10.90	4.09	9.68	57.34	3.13	.23	8.65	2.97	Do.
1757	Hominy, Green Diamond.	8.38	2.54	8.94	6.78	12.46	48.75	1.68	.23	5.88	4.36	2.77	9.76	7.40	13.60	53.22	1.83	.25	6.41	4.76	Do.
1758b	Hominy feed, Fru-man.	9.13	2.58	10.06	2.96	7.48	53.90	2.47	.21	6.84	4.37	2.84	11.07	3.26	8.23	59.32	2.72	.23	7.52	4.81	Do.
1761	...do feed...	7.89	2.79	9.44	5.49	12.50	47.69	2.58	.77	7.74	3.11	3.03	10.25	5.96	13.57	51.78	2.80	.83	8.40	3.37	Do.
1792c	...do...	9.14	2.09	10.25	3.37	8.19	49.50	1.25	.78	5.44	9.99	2.30	11.28	3.71	9.01	54.49	1.37	.86	5.99	10.99	Do.
1851	Hominy feed, Kidders.	11.83	2.38	9.38	3.94	8.64	47.75	.95	1.15	5.45	8.53	2.70	10.64	4.46	9.80	54.17	1.08	1.30	6.18	9.67	Do.
1892	Hominy feed	9.95	2.91	9.09	3.53	19.45	39.51	2.38	.79	6.08	6.31	3.23	10.10	3.92	21.59	43.87	2.65	.88	6.75	7.01	Do.
1913d	Hominy feed, Steam Ghed.	10.76	2.29	9.79	3.41	8.25	53.14	2.35	.37	5.78	3.86	2.57	10.97	3.82	9.24	59.56	2.63	.41	6.48	4.32	Do.

a See page 69. b See page 70. c See page 63. d See page 67.

BREWERY AND DISTILLERY PRODUCTS.

The average composition of seven samples of Ajax flakes, which are no more than distillers' dried grains, examined by the Connecticut Agricultural Experiment Station during 1904 and 1905,[a] together with the average analysis of six samples of malt sprouts from the same source and forty-two samples of brewers' dried grains examined by the New Jersey Agricultural Experiment Station,[b] are given in the following table:

TABLE 11.—*Average percentage analyses of brewery and distillery products.*

[Compiled.]

Description of sample.	Number of analyses.	Mois-ture.	Ash.	Protein.	Crude fiber.	Nitro-gen-free extract.	Fat.
Ajax flakes...................	7	7.19	2.10	31.49	12.55	32.94	13.74
Malt sprouts...................	6	9.94	5.83	25.15	11.40	45.98	1.71
Brewers' dried grains...............	42	8.9	3.70	23.90	13.20	43.30	7.00

An inspection of the samples of the distillers' grains examined in the Bureau of Chemistry (Table 12) shows that their protein content, except in one case, agrees well with the average. Although the fat content is low, there is nothing to indicate adulteration. Sample No. 1768 has a very low protein content as compared with the others.

The samples of brewers' dried grains are well up to the standard and evidently unadulterated. It is evident from the microscopical examination that No. 1819, while corresponding very closely in protein and fat content to brewers' dried grains, consists of a mixture of several different feeding materials.

All samples of malt sprouts examined agree well with the standard and show no indications of adulteration. The sucrose and reducing-sugar figures vary considerably, but this is to be expected from the nature of the goods.

---

[a] Report of the Connecticut Agricultural Experiment Station for 1904, Part V, 1905, Part III.

[b] Twenty-second Annual Report of the New Jersey Agricultural Experiment Station.

TABLE 12.—*Brewery and distillery products (percentage composition).*

Serial No.	Name and brand.	Moisture.	Calculated to basis of original sample.									Calculated to a moisture-free basis.									Raw materials identified by microscopic examination.
			Ash.	Crude protein.	Crude fiber.	Pentosan.	Starch.	Sucrose.	Reducing sugars.	Ether extract.	Undetermined.	Ash.	Crude protein.	Crude fiber.	Pentosan.	Starch.	Sucrose.	Reducing sugars.	Ether extract.	Undetermined.	
1589a	Distillers' dried grains, Fourex.	5.89	1.98	34.88	13.04	17.94	8.29	.0	.0	9.16	8.82	2.10	37.07	13.86	19.06	8.81	.0	.0	9.73	9.37	Distillers' grains (corn, rye, and barley).
1695a	...do...	6.22	2.44	32.19	18.01	18.56	2.79	.0	.0	11.35	8.44	2.60	34.35	19.20	19.79	2.98	.0	.0	12.08	9.00	Do.
1990a	...do...	8.70	1.67	32.75	18.42	18.81	6.50	.0	.0	5.42	7.73	1.82	35.90	20.17	20.60	7.11	.0	.0	5.93	8.47	Do.
	Average...	6.94	2.03	33.27	16.49	18.44	5.86	.00	.00	8.64	8.33	2.17	35.77	17.74	19.82	6.30	.00	.00	9.25	8.95	
1606	Distillers' corn grains, Blue Ribbon.	5.19	1.91	31.00	14.61	18.95	15.20	.0	.0	12.11	1.03	2.01	32.71	15.40	19.99	16.03	.0	.0	12.77	1.09	Distillers' grains (corn and barley), smartweed.
1925	...do...	9.59	2.36	34.30	12.75	16.64	12.24	.0	.0	7.55	4.57	2.61	37.92	14.13	18.39	13.54	.0	.0	8.35	5.06	Distillers' grains (corn and barley).
1985	...do...	10.43	1.91	32.42	13.68	17.62	11.99	.0	.0	7.49	4.46	2.13	36.20	15.28	19.67	13.38	.0	.0	8.36	4.98	Do.
	Average...	8.40	2.06	32.58	13.68	17.74	13.14	.0	.0	9.05	3.35	2.22	35.61	14.94	19.35	14.33	.0	.0	9.83	3.72	
1614b	Ajax flakes...	4.54	1.75	30.88	14.88	21.20	6.65	.0	.0	11.84	8.26	1.83	32.35	15.59	22.21	6.97	.0	.0	12.40	8.65	Distillers' grains (corn, barley, and possibly some rye).
1789b	...do...	7.50	2.03	32.63	14.03	20.30	3.76	.0	.0	8.73	11.02	2.19	35.28	15.17	21.94	4.06	.0	.0	9.44	11.91	Distillers' grains (corn, barley, and trace of rye).
1843b	...do...	7.51	2.31	34.90	12.25	17.83	6.26	.0	.0	8.96	9.98	2.50	37.69	13.24	19.33	6.76	.0	.0	9.68	10.80	Do.
	Average...	6.52	2.03	32.80	13.72	19.78	5.56	.0	.0	9.84	9.75	2.17	35.11	14.67	21.16	5.93	.0	.0	10.51	10.45	
1768a	Biles rye grains...	7.42	1.98	19.13	12.69	31.71	12.65	.0	.15	5.79	8.48	2.13	20.66	13.71	34.27	13.66	.0	.16	6.25	9.16	Distillers' grains (barley and rye).
1530	Brewers' dried grains.	6.65	5.89	24.50	14.23	22.67	10.71	.0	.87	5.52	8.96	6.31	26.25	15.24	24.28	11.47	.0	.93	5.91	9.60	Brewers' grains (barley tissues).
1565	...do...	4.99	3.67	26.50	15.46	23.19	10.88	.0	.18	6.43	8.70	3.86	27.89	16.27	24.41	11.45	.0	.19	6.77	9.16	Do.
	Average...	5.82	4.78	25.50	14.85	22.93	10.80	.0	.52	5.97	8.83	5.08	27.07	15.76	24.35	11.46	.0	.56	6.34	9.33	

a See page 63. b See page 64.

TABLE 12.—Brewery and distillery products (percentage composition)—Continued.

Serial No.	Name and brand.	Moisture.	Calculated to basis of original sample.									Calculated to a moisture-free basis.									Raw materials identified by microscopic examination.
			Ash.	Crude protein.	Crude fiber.	Pentosan.	Starch.	Sucrose.	Reducing sugars.	Ether extract.	Undetermined.	Ash.	Crude protein.	Crude fiber.	Pentosan.	Starch.	Sucrose.	Reducing sugars.	Ether extract.	Undetermined.	
1819a	Union grains	9.60	7.37	23.51	9.12	13.23	19.23	1.41	2.29	6.81	7.43	8.15	26.02	10.09	14.63	21.27	1.56	2.53	7.54	8.21	Distillers' grains, barley sprouts, hominy feed, trace of oats, cottonseed meal, W. P. No. 3, pigweed, linseed meal. Sprouts, barley hulls.
1534	Malt sprouts	5.59	5.73	25.44	13.02	15.87	8.46	1.87	13.36	1.04	9.62	6.07	26.95	13.79	16.81	8.96	1.98	14.15	1.10	10.19	Do.
1821	...do	13.09	5.98	25.78	12.23	15.83	3.98	2.52	9.24	.74	10.61	6.89	29.67	14.07	18.20	4.58	2.90	10.63	.85	12.21	
	Average	9.34	5.86	25.61	12.62	15.85	6.22	2.19	11.30	.89	10.12	6.48	28.31	13.93	17.51	6.77	2.44	12.39	.97	11.20	Malt sprouts.
1524	Malt sprouts	8.84	5.81	23.81	13.16	16.25	7.40	2.78	13.35	1.19	7.41	6.37	26.12	14.44	17.83	8.12	3.05	14.64	1.31	8.12	Malt sprouts, trace of oats and smartweed seed.
501	...do	7.22	5.79	27.13	14.25	17.39	8.52	1.44	7.17	.94	10.15	6.24	29.25	15.36	18.74	9.18	1.55	7.73	1.01	10.94	
1727	...do	8.47	6.06	25.56	13.31	18.65	7.05	2.93	5.60	.81	11.56	6.62	27.93	14.54	20.34	7.70	3.20	6.12	.88	12.63	Malt sprouts, char- la.
1735	...do	9.57	5.66	25.19	12.00	15.60	7.40	4.43	11.59	.73	7.83	6.26	27.86	13.27	17.25	8.18	4.90	12.81	.81	8.66	Malt sprouts, smartweed seed.
1924	...do	11.08	6.33	28.64	13.82	16.24	3.65	2.67	6.19	.85	10.53	7.12	32.22	15.54	18.26	4.10	3.00	6.96	.96	11.84	Do.

a See page 62.

WHEAT FEEDS.

The average composition of wheat flour, middlings, shorts, and bran as given by Jenkins and Winton [a] is as follows:

TABLE 13.—*Average percentage composition of wheat flour, middlings, shorts, and bran.*

[Compiled.]

Description of sample.	Number of analyses.	Moisture.	Ash.	Crude fiber.	Crude protein.	Crude fat.	Nitrogen-free extract.
Flour	20	12.4	0.5	0.2	10.8	1.1	75.00
Middlings	32	12.1	3.3	4.6	15.6	4.0	60.40
Shorts	12	11.8	4.6	7.4	14.9	4.5	56.80
Bran	88	11.9	5.8	9.0	15.4	4.0	53.90

The average composition of middlings and bran from winter and spring wheat sold in Connecticut [b] in 1905 is as follows:

TABLE 14.—*Average percentage composition of middlings and bran.*

[Compiled.]

Description of sample.	Number of analyses.	Moisture.	Ash.	Crude fiber.	Crude protein.	Crude fat.	Nitrogen-free extract.
Bran, winter wheat	9	10.45	6.73	8.77	15.19	4.56	54.28
Bran, spring wheat	16	10.90	6.31	10.54	14.06	4.70	53.49
Middlings, winter wheat	4	10.97	4.28	5.60	16.44	4.52	58.19
Middlings, spring wheat	16	11.34	4.67	6.03	16.78	4.84	56.34

The samples of Red Dog examined (Table 15) are evidently true to name, and, as we would expect in a low grade of flour, contain a larger amount of protein than would appear in a high-grade flour.

All of the samples except No. 1847 contain about the quantity of crude fiber that would be expected. In No. 1847 the fiber is high, but the high starch content, together with the microscopic examination, shows that this is not due to an excess of hulls.

The samples of middlings examined all contain a quantity of protein agreeing well with the average. The tendency to high contents of ash, crude fiber, and pentosans, and to a low content of starch in samples Nos. 1834 and 1937 would indicate that they more closely resembled bran than middlings as regards a number of their constituents.

All samples of bran examined appear to be unadulterated and to correspond quite closely to the average composition for bran as given in Table 13.

[a] Loc. cit.
[b] Report of the Connecticut Agricultural Experiment Station, 1905, Part III.

It would appear from the analyses of bran and middlings, given in Table 14, that sufficient distinction is not made in the trade between these two products. What one manufacturer calls bran, another calls middlings, so that there is not the clear-cut difference there should be in the average composition of these two classes of goods sold on the American market.

Samples Nos. 1617 and 1703 are two samples of the same goods purchased at different places. The analyses, both chemical and microscopical, show that they are very different substances.

TABLE 15.—*Wheat feeds* (percentage composition).

Serial No.	Name and brand.	Moisture.	Calculated to basis of original sample.									Calculated to a moisture-free basis.									Raw materials identified by microscopical examination.
			Ash.	Crude protein.	Crude fiber.	Pentosan.	Starch.	Sucrose.	Reducing sugars.	Ether extract.	Undetermined.	Ash.	Crude protein.	Crude fiber.	Pentosan.	Starch.	Sucrose.	Reducing sugars.	Ether extract.	Undetermined.	
1833	Red Dog (G)	11.44	3.21	18.54	2.37	5.42	43.53	3.38	2.29	1.68	8.14	3.62	20.93	2.68	6.12	49.17	3.81	2.59	1.89	9.19	W. P. No. 3, rich in endosperm.
1847	Red Dog (H)	12.25	1.18	13.91	10.63	3.52	47.46	1.63	.76	2.10	6.55	1.34	15.85	12.11	4.01	54.11	1.86	.87	2.39	7.46	Do.
1910	Red Dog, Cornet XXX.	11.83	3.77	19.32	3.02	11.30	34.55	3.69	2.56	5.36	4.60	4.27	21.92	3.42	12.82	39.18	4.19	2.90	6.08	5.22	W. P. No. 3.
1917	Red Dog, and standard middlings.	15.24	3.65	19.37	2.50	8.12	33.47	3.65	1.76	4.78	6.46	4.30	22.85	2.95	9.58	40.69	4.30	2.07	5.04	7.62	Do.
1834		11.12	5.38	16.88	11.26	21.42	15.00	3.56	2.18	2.87	10.33	6.06	18.99	12.67	24.11	16.87	4.00	2.46	3.22	11.62	W. P. No. 2, corn cockle, smartweed.
1841	Flouy middlings...	10.00	4.28	18.19	5.28	14.90	28.01	4.46	2.02	4.84	8.02	4.75	20.21	5.86	16.56	31.15	4.95	2.24	5.37	8.91	W. P. No. 2.
1894	Middlings......	12.44	3.09	17.12	5.60	9.14	41.97	2.34	1.92	1.71	4.07	3.50	19.53	6.41	10.45	47.96	2.67	2.19	1.96	5.33	Do.
1895	Flour tilings...	9.20	4.95	19.62	5.97	16.14	31.05	5.14	2.20	4.47	1.26	5.45	21.60	6.58	17.78	34.18	5.66	2.43	2.43	1.40	Do.
1937	Standard middlings.	11.60	5.25	16.55	13.44	22.30	21.21	4.09	1.80	3.52	.24	5.94	18.71	15.19	25.23	24.00	4.63	2.04	3.98	.28	Do.
1844	Bran (H)	11.61	5.76	16.35	7.31	19.25	21.72	4.28	1.37	3.91	8.44	6.51	18.49	8.27	21.77	24.60	4.84	1.55	4.42	9.55	W. P. No. 1.
1953	Bran	11.93	7.07	16.63	10.33	22.09	15.18	3.99	1.41	3.93	7.44	8.03	18.88	11.73	25.10	17.23	4.52	1.60	4.46	8.45	W. P. No. 1, smartwd. corn cockle, weed.
1961	Ogilvie's bran...	9.31	6.44	15.23	10.70	16.84	22.73	3.64	1.78	3.39	9.94	7.10	16.80	11.80	18.57	25.04	4.01	1.96	3.76	10.96	W. P. No. 1.
1964	Holliday bran...	11.59	6.08	15.40	7.99	19.81	21.54	4.43	1.13	3.51	8.52	6.87	17.41	9.03	22.41	24.39	5.01	1.28	3.96	9.64	W. P. No. 1, smartweed.
1982	Bran (L)(K)	14.80	5.64	14.87	9.40	20.77	17.59	3.31	1.37	3.25	9.00	6.61	17.46	11.03	24.39	20.65	3.88	1.60	3.82	10.56	W. P. No. 1.
1591	Standard bran, middlings and flour.	8.71	4.96	17.44	6.65	17.18	27.08	4.43	1.58	4.67	7.30	5.43	19.11	7.28	18.82	29.67	4.85	1.73	5.11	8.00	W. P. No. 1 and No. 3.
1607	Monarch ground wt feed.	7.81	6.08	14.50	8.28	18.71	33.00	5.56	1.33	4.69	.04	6.59	15.72	8.98	20.30	35.81	6.03	1.44	5.09	.04	W. P. No. 1, corn cockle.
1617	Rye wheat feed.	8.87	5.77	15.75	7.81	19.56	23.32	5.29	.94	4.47	8.22	6.33	17.28	8.57	21.46	25.60	5.80	1.03	4.91	9.02	W. P. No. 1.
1703	...do...	6.46	2.34	12.81	5.05	12.69	48.09	1.50	2.19	3.08	5.79	2.50	13.70	5.40	13.57	51.42	1.60	2.33	3.29	6.19	W. P. No. 2, corn cockle,
	Average...	7.67	4.05	14.28	6.43	16.13	35.71	3.39	1.56	3.77	7.01	4.42	15.49	6.98	17.52	38.51	3.70	1.68	4.10	7.60	
1619ᵃ	Standard wheat feed.	8.81	5.59	16.50	7.97	19.29	26.77	2.05	1.57	4.09	7.36	6.13	18.09	8.74	21.15	29.36	2.25	1.72	4.49	8.07	W. P. Nos. 1, 2, and 3, trace of corn cob.
1774	Winter wheat mixed feed.	8.65	4.74	15.81	7.56	19.43	30.19	3.79	1.56	3.60	4.67	5.18	17.31	8.27	21.27	33.06	4.15	1.71	3.94	5.11	W. P. Nos. 3, corn ruffbs
1836	Shredded wheat....	9.09	1.91	11.26	4.21	6.81	55.22	1.97	.22	8.80	.51	2.10	12.38	4.63	7.49	60.75	2.16	.25	9.68	.36	whole wheat

ᵃ See p. 69.

The average composition of ground whole oats, oat hulls, and oat straw, as given by Winton and Jenkins,[a] is as follows:

TABLE 16.—*Average percentage composition of ground whole oats, oat hulls, and oat straw.*

[Compiled.]

Description of sample.	Number of analyses.	Mois- ture.	Ash.	Crude fiber.	Crude protein.	Fat.	Nitro- gen-free extract.
Whole oats	30	11.0	3.0	9.5	11.8	5.0	59.7
Oat hulls	6	7.3	6.7	31.6	2.9	1.1	50.4
Oat straw	12	9.2	5.1	37.0	4.0	2.3	42.4

Considering the samples of oat feeds reported in Table 17 as a whole it is at once evident that most of them are composed largely of oat hulls, and consequently have a low feeding value. Samples Nos. 1494, 1962, 1505, 1705, 1499, 1518, 1914, 1934, and 1941, from their high ash content (with the exception of No. 1518), their low protein, starch, and fat content, the very high crude fiber and pentosan content, and the microscopical examination, show that they are composed very largely of hulls, while sample No. 1631, labeled as "ground oats," evidently contains hulls in considerable excess. Sample No. 1838 is labeled "oat feed," and in chemical composition corresponds quite closely to ground whole oats, but a microscopical examination shows it to be a mixture of oats and corn with a small amount of some other cereal, probably barley. Sample No. 1888, both from its chemical composition and the microscopical examination, would appear to be composed of ground oats.

---

[a] Loc. cit.

TABLE 17.—Oat feeds (percentage composition).

Serial No.	Name and brand.	Moisture.	Calculated to basis of original sample.									Calculated to a moisture-free basis.									Raw materials identified by microscopical examination.
			Ash.	Crude protein.	Crude fiber.	Pentosan.	Starch.	Sucrose.	Reducing sugars.	Ether extract.	Undetermined.	Ash.	Crude protein.	Crude fiber.	Pentosan.	Starch.	Sucrose.	Reducing sugars.	Ether extract.	Undetermined.	
1494	Oat feed, Vim....	6.16	6.44	8.00	25.32	28.17	13.72	0.84	0.51	2.52	8.32	6.86	8.53	26.98	30.02	14.62	0.90	0.54	2.69	8.86	Cracked and ground oats, hulls, possibly in excess of normal.
1962	.....do.........	7.56	4.89	3.89	27.77	31.09	16.26	.38	.29	1.58	6.29	5.29	4.21	30.05	33.64	17.59	.41	.31	1.70	6.81	Largely oat hulls, yellow dock seed.
	Average......	6.86	5.67	5.94	26.55	29.63	14.99	.61	.40	2.05	7.30	6.07	6.37	28.51	31.83	16.10	.66	.43	2.19	7.84	
1505	Oat feed, Royal...	6.46	7.57	5.94	24.63	28.07	18.28	.0	1.32	1.63	6.10	8.09	6.35	26.33	30.02	19.54	.0	1.41	1.74	6.52	Oat product, with excess of hulls.
1705	.....do.........	7.12	5.99	5.81	27.15	31.81	10.97	.63	.14	1.86	8.52	6.45	6.26	29.23	34.25	11.81	.68	.15	2.00	9.17	Mostly oat hulls.
	, Average...	6.79	6.78	5.88	25.89	29.94	14.63	.31	.73	1.74	7.31	7.27	6.30	27.78	32.14	15.68	.34	.77	1.87	7.85	
1499	Oat feed, X	6.39	5.94	7.75	24.67	26.23	16.59	.70	.45	2.97	8.31	6.35	8.28	26.35	28.02	17.72	.75	.48	3.17	8.88	Ground oats, with possible excess of hulls; charlock, smartweed, foxtail, curled dock, linseed meal.
1518	Oat feed, Cream..	6.68	3.25	5.19	26.05	24.55	22.79	.13	.93	1.49	8.94	3.48	5.56	27.92	26.31	24.42	.14	.99	1.60	9.58	Ground oats, with possible excess of hulls.
1631	Ground oats......	6.70	4.74	7.56	18.49	22.57	28.20	.29	1.34	2.67	7.44	5.08	8.10	19.82	24.19	30.23	.31	1.44	2.86	7.97	Ground oats largely composed of oat hulls.
1838	Oat feed, Schumackers.	11.42	3.92	10.10	10.07	14.65	39.21	1.66	1.35	3.12	4.50	4.42	11.41	11.39	16.54	44.24	1.88	1.52	3.52	5.08	Ground oats, corn, some other cereal, probably barley.
1888	Oat middlings....	8.99	4.12	17.74	5.79	8.08	36.51	2.60	1.08	6.45	8.64	4.53	19.48	6.36	8.88	40.11	2.86	1.19	7.09	9.50	Ground oats, low in amount of hulls.
1914	Oat feed, O. F	7.98	5.31	6.55	23.59	26.59	19.40	.30	1.01	1.43	7.84	5.77	7.12	25.63	28.89	21.08	.33	1.10	1.56	8.52	Mostly oat hulls.
1934	Oat feed......	8.95	5.39	5.85	25.26	26.71	17.88	.78	.25	1.81	7.12	5.92	6.42	27.73	29.35	19.64	.86	.27	1.99	7.82	Mostly oat hulls, smartweed.
1941	Oat feed (F)......	9.70	4.92	5.68	24.76	26.91	17.34	.76	.13	1.87	7.93	5.45	6.29	27.42	29.81	19.20	.83	.14	2.07	8.79	Mostly oat hulls.

CORN AND OAT FEEDS.

Under this heading have been classified not only the products labeled "corn and oat feed" but also chop feed, provender, feeds bearing names that would indicate that they were composed of corn and oats, and feeds which a microscopical examination has shown to be composed chiefly of corn and oats.

The average composition of corn and oats, and of ground corn and oat feeds, as they appear on the market, is given in the following table:[a]

TABLE 18.—*Average percentage composition of corn and oat feeds.*

[Compiled.]

Constituents.	Number of analyses.	Mois-ture.	Ash.	Crude fiber.	Crude protein.	Crude fat.	Nitro-gen-free extract.
Corn..........................	15	15.4	1.3	1.5	9.1	4.1	68.6
Oats........................	20	11.4	3.1	9.9	11.3	4.8	59.5
Ground corn and oats............	38	11.9	2.2	4.0	9.7	4.5	67.7

On the whole it may be said that a large number of the corn and oat feeds and the samples labeled ground corn and oats reported in Table 19 are unsatisfactory in their composition, adulteration with hulls being indicated in many cases by the high ash, crude fiber, and pentosan content and the small amount of starch present. Even when no adulteration with hulls is indicated a number of the samples show by their low protein and fat content that they are made up of inferior grades of corn and oats. In some cases a wheat product, such as bran, middlings, or red-dog flour, has been added, probably for the purpose of raising the protein content.

It is unnecessary to mention all the individual cases of apparent adulteration in Table 19. A comparison of the analyses with the average given in Table 18 and an inspection of the microscopical examination show at once what samples are to be rejected.

The "chop feeds" and "provenders" are open to the same criticism as the "corn and oat feeds," but perhaps to a somewhat less extent. Some evidently contain an excess of hulls, while others are made from cereals of poor quality. Only a very few of them are entirely above suspicion. From the amount of weed seed found in some of these samples it is evident that screenings were used in their preparation or that they were made from very inferior grains.

Samples Nos. 1604, 1933, and 1958 have just about the composition that would be expected in a mixture of corn and oats without an excess of hulls.

---

[a] New Jersey Agr. Exper. Stat., Twenty-second Annual Report, 1901.

TABLE 19.—*Corn and oat feeds (percentage composition).*

Serial No.	Name and brand	Moisture	Ash	Crude protein	Crude fiber	Pentosan	Starch	Sucrose	Reducing sugars	Ether extract	Undetermined	Ash	Crude protein	Crude fiber	Pentosan	Starch	Sucrose	Reducing sugars	Ether extract	Undetermined	Raw materials identified by microscopical examination.
			Calculated to basis of original sample.									Calculated to a moisture-free basis.									
1477	Corn and oat feed, Boss.	7.88	6.11	7.81	14.39	18.30	34.40	1.46	0.29	2.07	7.29	6.63	8.48	15.62	19.87	37.35	1.58	0.31	2.25	7.91	Ground corn and oats, excess of hulls.
1817	do	11.70	6.70	8.52	11.02	15.88	33.22	.71	1.16	3.00	8.09	7.58	9.64	12.49	17.98	37.62	.81	1.32	3.40	9.16	Ground corn and oats.
	Average	9.79	6.40	8.17	12.71	17.09	33.81	1.08	.72	2.54	7.69	7.10	9.06	14.06	18.93	37.49	1.19	.81	2.82	8.54	
1487	Corn and oat feed, De-Fi.	7.43	3.92	9.38	14.16	19.18	32.20	1.48	.94	2.75	8.56	4.23	10.13	15.29	20.72	34.80	1.60	1.01	2.97	9.25	Ground corn and oats (oat hulls in excess), W. P. No.1.
1977	do	10.81	4.90	9.60	13.85	18.71	29.44	2.44	.46	2.28	7.51	5.50	10.77	15.53	20.98	33.00	2.73	.51	2.56	8.42	Ground corn and oats, W. P. No.1, large excess of oat hulls.
	Average	9.12	4.41	9.49	14.01	18.95	30.82	1.96	.70	2.51	8.03	4.86	10.45	15.41	20.85	33.90	2.16	.76	2.77	8.84	
1496a	Corn and oat feed, Arrow.	10.28	1.70	8.44	3.68	7.51	62.59	.88	1.27	2.98	.67	1.89	9.41	4.08	8.37	69.76	.98	1.42	3.32	.77	Ground corn and oats, trace of buckwheat hulls.
1781	do	21.27	1.26	8.02	2.43	5.56	53.16	.11	.56	1.74	5.89	1.60	10.19	3.09	7.06	67.52	.14	.71	2.21	7.48	Ground corn and oats.
	Average	15.78	1.48	8.23	3.05	6.54	57.88	.49	.91	2.36	3.28	1.74	9.80	3.59	7.72	68.64	.56	1.06	2.76	4.13	
1504	Corn and oat feed, Excel snr.	8.24	4.06	9.81	11.84	16.09	36.28	.97	.91	3.52	8.28	4.42	10.69	12.90	17.53	39.54	1.07	.99	3.84	9.02	Ground corn and oats, trace of weed seed.
1599	do	6.91	3.91	9.63	10.10	15.36	35.40	1.59	.91	6.24	9.95	4.20	10.34	10.85	16.50	38.04	1.71	.98	6.70	10.68	Ground corn and oats, trace of pigweed seed.
	Average	7.58	3.98	9.72	10.97	15.73	35.84	1.28	.91	4.88	9.11	4.31	10.51	11.88	17.02	38.79	1.39	.98	5.27	9.85	
1558	Corn and oat feed, Victor.	8.49	3.99	8.38	10.66	14.54	46.09	.99	.43	3.38	3.05	4.36	9.16	11.65	15.89	50.37	1.08	.47	3.69	3.33	Ground corn and oats (excess of hulls), curled dock, smartweed.
1762	do	8.84	3.70	8.88	10.68	14.60	46.87	1.68	.75	3.84	.16	4.06	9.74	11.72	16.02	51.42	1.84	.82	4.21	.17	Ground corn and oats, trace of wheat product, charlock.
	Average	8.67	3.84	8.63	10.67	14.57	46.48	1.33	.59	3.61	1.61	4.21	9.45	11.68	15.96	50.90	1.46	.64	3.95	1.75	
1587	Corn and oat feed, Niagara.	8.70	2.18	8.50	6.21	9.91	51.47	.69	.83	3.71	7.80	2.39	9.31	6.80	10.86	56.38	.75	.91	4.06	8.54	Ground corn and oats, curled dock.
1710	do	8.44	3.09	7.44	14.91	23.64	35.53	.63	.94	2.89	2.49	3.37	8.12	16.28	25.82	38.81	.69	1.03	3.16	2.72	Ground corn and oats, excess of corn and oat hulls, charlock.
1740	do	7.84	3.42	6.94	15.03	21.30	34.96	.68	.55	2.24	7.04	3.71	7.53	16.31	23.11	37.94	.73	.60	2.43	7.64	Ground corn and oats, excess of corn and oat hulls.
	Average	8.33	2.90	7.63	12.05	18.28	40.65	.67	.77	2.95	5.77	3.16	8.32	13.13	19.93	44.38	.72	.84	3.22	6.30	

a See p. 68.

TABLE 19.—*Corn and oat feeds (percentage composition)*—Continued.

Serial No.	Name and brand.	Calculated to basis of original sample.										Calculated to a moisture-free basis.									Raw materials identified by microscopical examination.
		Moisture.	Ash.	Crude protein.	Crude fiber.	Pentosan.	Starch.	Sucrose.	Reducing sugars.	Ether extract.	Undetermined.	Ash.	Crude protein.	Crude fiber.	Pentosan.	Starch.	Sucrose.	Reducing sugars.	Ether extract.	Undetermined.	
1625a	Corn and oat feed, XXX.	8.80	3.28	9.81	9.33	13.74	40.40	1.59	1.18	4.15	7.72	3.60	10.76	10.23	15.07	44.30	1.74	1.29	4.55	8.46	Ground corn and oats, small amount of W. P. No. 3, corn cockle.
1741a	...do.......	7.81	3.42	9.63	12.51	18.61	34.84	1.39	1.49	3.78	6.52	3.71	10.45	13.57	20.18	37.80	1.51	1.61	4.10	7.07	Ground corn and oats, W. P. No. 3.
1922a	...do.......	14.80	3.20	9.04	9.27	16.93	33.01	1.09	1.94	3.29	7.43	3.76	10.61	10.88	19.86	38.75	1.28	2.28	3.86	8.72	Ground corn and oats, W. P. No. 2.
	Average.......	10.47	3.30	9.49	10.37	16.43	36.08	1.36	1.54	3.74	7.22	3.69	10.61	11.56	18.37	40.28	1.51	1.73	4.17	8.08	
1713b	Ground corn and oats.	15.86	1.88	10.37	2.93	6.67	50.34	1.44	1.39	1.97	7.15	2.22	12.33	3.48	7.93	59.85	1.70	1.65	2.34	8.50	Ground corn and oats, W. P. No. 2, small amount of smartweed.
1474	Corn and oat feed, Dandy.	8.61	2.59	8.66	7.87	13.65	48.27	1.47	1.23	4.11	3.54	2.83	9.46	8.61	14.94	52.81	1.61	1.35	4.50	3.89	Ground corn and oats, trace of wheat, smartweed.
1482	Corn and oat feed.	8.76	3.17	7.50	11.84	16.18	41.25	.80	.34	2.63	7.53	3.47	8.22	12.97	17.73	45.20	.88	.37	2.88	8.28	Ground corn and oats.
1492	Ground corn and oats.	8.67	3.59	9.31	9.02	11.78	45.94	.93	.85	2.41	7.50	3.93	10.19	9.88	12.90	50.30	1.02	.93	2.65	8.20	Ground corn and oats, trace of rye, smartweed.
1508	...do.......	9.06	2.09	10.69	4.85	17.48	50.53	.97	.96	3.23	.15	2.30	11.75	5.33	19.22	55.58	1.06	1.05	3.55	.16	Ground corn and oats, W. P. No. 1, smartweed, rough pigweed, Brassica (sp.).
1520	Corn meal and chop feed.	10.35	2.32	8.06	4.71	8.21	54.28	.15	1.16	3.26	7.50	2.58	8.99	5.25	9.16	60.56	.17	1.29	3.64	8.36	Ground corn and oats.
1511	Ground corn and oats.	9.87	1.84	9.19	4.40	8.30	52.03	.89	.76	3.24	9.48	2.04	10.19	4.88	9.21	57.75	.99	.84	3.59	10.51	Ground corn and oats, smartweed.
1526	...do.......	9.53	1.79	8.38	4.91	8.82	58.21	.79	.74	2.69	4.14	1.98	9.26	5.43	9.75	64.34	.87	.82	2.97	4.58	Ground corn and oats.
1544	...do.......	9.69	2.44	10.31	5.92	9.40	54.00	.82	1.32	2.97	3.13	2.70	11.41	6.56	10.41	59.79	.91	1.46	3.29	3.47	Coarsely ground corn, oats, and some barley.
1548	...do.......	9.15	2.46	8.00	6.90	10.40	52.97	.58	.90	2.35	6.29	2.71	8.81	7.59	11.45	58.31	.64	.99	2.58	6.92	Ground corn and oats, smartweed, yellow dock.
1549	...do.......	7.35	3.31	9.06	8.93	14.40	42.82	1.46	1.15	5.02	6.50	3.57	9.78	9.64	15.54	46.18	1.58	1.23	5.42	7.06	Ground corn and oats, weed seeds.
1561	Corn and oat feed, Anchor.	7.93	4.98	8.75	13.45	17.33	37.68	.68	1.48	2.19	5.53	5.41	9.50	14.61	18.82	40.92	.74	1.61	2.38	6.01	Ground corn, oats, and W. P. No. 1 and No.2.
1566	Ground corn and oats.	8.68	1.98	9.06	4.58	9.53	57.73	.94	1.01	3.50	2.99	2.17	9.92	5.01	10.44	63.22	1.03	1.11	3.83	3.27	Ground corn and oats, smartweed.
1598	Corn and oat chop.	7.23	3.69	8.25	11.73	15.99	39.19	1.43	.86	3.76	7.87	3.98	8.87	12.64	17.23	42.29	1.54	.92	4.04	8.46	Ground corn and oats.
1603	Corn and oat feed, Capital.	7.30	4.19	6.63	19.14	22.36	28.18	.88	.70	2.39	8.23	4.52	7.15	20.65	24.12	30.39	.95	.76	2.58	8.88	Cracked corn and oats with trace of rye, oats mostly as hulls.
1699c	Ground corn and oats.	20.34	2.55	8.98	5.65	8.77	43.58	.34	.68	2.89	6.18	3.20	11.29	7.09	11.02	54.77	.43	.85	3.59	7.76	Coarsely ground corn and oats (excess of hulls), trace of wheat.

No.	Description															
1731	Corn and oat feed.	8.33	2.54	8.44	8.52	0.94	4.76	.89	2.68	9.21	2.77	9.21	9.29	11.93	52.11	.98	.75	2.92	10.04
1475	Corn and oat chop.	10.01	2.74	6.94	8.72	12.29	51.79	.58	2.58	3.49	3.04	7.71	9.69	13.66	57.55	.04	.95	2.88	3.88
136	....do....	9.36	2.71	10.06	5.34	9.43	52.50	1.09	3.61	4.07	2.99	11.11	5.89	10.40	57.92	1.20	2.02	3.98	4.49
697	Chop feed, Niagara.	16.49	3.25	9.29	7.35	1.02	42.69	.36	2.29	5.44	2.89	11.12	8.81	13.19	51.13	.43	2.18	2.74	6.51
1701d	Corn and oat chop, No. 2.	8.86	2.89	7.31	11.01	14.42	43.31	1.18	2.29	7.39	3.17	8.02	12.06	15.82	47.53	1.47	1.29	2.51	8.11
1702	Corn and oat chop.	7.69	3.76	10.13	9.38	12.19	44.12	1.33	3.34	2.10	4.07	10.97	10.16	13.20	47.81	1.44	1.04	3.62	7.09
1709	....do....	19.05	2.44	9.16	5.43	7.37	46.71	.42	2.52	6.00	3.02	11.31	6.70	9.11	57.71	.52	1.10	3.12	7.41
1752		20.18	2.41	7.60	5.20	16.27	45.52	.14	1.91	.02	3.02	9.51	6.51	20.39	57.04	.18	.94	2.39	.02
1760		8.81	2.31	7.31	9.76	6.77	54.32	.80	2.31	6.97	2.53	8.02	10.70	7.42	59.58	.88	.70	2.53	7.64
1777		7.90	3.47	9.38	10.14	16.17	38.20	1.13	5.49	6.51	3.77	10.18	11.01	17.56	41.47	1.23	1.75	5.96	7.07
1786	Do.	9.17	2.02	7.69	10.17	15.31	45.00	.63	2.64	5.39	2.88	8.46	11.19	16.85	49.57	.69	1.52	2.91	5.93
1577	fed, Monⁿⁿⁿ.	7.85	3.64	7.00	13.87	18.60	41.75	1.08	2.16	3.18	3.95	7.60	15.05	20.19	45.31	1.17	.94	2.34	3.45
624	....do....	9.29	3.21	8.75	10.47	15.35	39.82	1.27	3.63	6.83	3.54	9.65	11.54	16.92	43.90	1.40	4.52	4.00	7.53
	Average....	8.57	3.42	7.88	12.17	16.98	40.79	1.17	2.89	5.01	3.74	8.62	13.30	18.56	44.61	1.28	1.23	3.17	5.49
1510c	at pov-ⁿⁿⁿ.	8.64	3.28	7.56	11.33	15.20	39.30	.39	2.42	10.57	3.59	8.27	12.40	16.64	43.02	.43	1.43	2.65	11.57
921		9.25	3.54	7.63	11.66	14.74	36.75	.92	2.32	12.59	3.90	8.41	12.85	16.24	40.50	.66	1.01	2.56	13.87
1704c		8.72	3.67	6.75	15.27	18.30	37.31	.60	2.02	6.78	4.02	7.39	16.73	20.05	40.88	.04	.66	2.21	7.42
1818	Provender....	12.69	3.52	7.82	12.12	15.36	38.78	.67	1.55	7.04	4.04	8.96	13.88	17.59	44.43	.76	.51	1.77	8.00
916	....do....	11.65	3.70	8.37	14.31	16.76	35.46	1.27	2.80	5.38	4.18	9.48	16.20	18.97	40.14	1.43	.34	3.17	6.09
134		8.96	4.00	7.81	9.11	10.44	49.97	.95	2.88	4.10	4.39	8.58	10.01	11.47	54.92	1.04	1.93	3.16	4.50
1555	....do....	7.89	3.63	6.56	15.49	18.77	35.42	.81	2.52	8.48	3.94	7.12	16.82	20.38	38.46	.88	.47	2.73	9.20
1569	....do....	8.61	2.41	9.25	15.54	9.25	48.29	.28	3.59	1.71	2.64	10.12	17.00	10.12	52.84	.31	1.17	3.93	1.87

a See page 63. b See page 66. c See page 68. d See page 65.

TABLE 19.—*Corn and oat feeds (percentage composition)*—Continued.

Serial No.	Name and brand.	Moisture.	Calculated to basis of original sample.									Calculated to a moisture-free basis.									Raw materials identified by microscopical examination.
			Ash.	Crude protein.	Crude fiber.	Pentosan.	Starch.	Sucrose.	Reducing sugars.	Ether extract.	Undetermined.	Ash.	Crude protein.	Crude fiber.	Pentosan.	Starch.	Sucrose.	Reducing sugars.	Ether extract.	Undetermined.	
1570	Ground feed	8.92	3.45	9.25	8.92	13.76	44.40	0.41	0.89	1.92	8.08	3.79	10.15	9.79	15.11	48.75	0.45	0.98	2.11	8.87	Ground corn and oats, trace of wheat product, and rose seed.
1765	6 mm n feed	8.49	3.36	8.75	8.45	16.16	39.88	1.26	1.09	4.33	8.23	3.67	9.56	9.23	17.66	43.59	1.38	1.19	4.73	8.99	Ground corn and oats.
1604a	"00" yellow feed	8.33	3.31	11.50	6.59	12.89	42.92	1.04	2.18	5.23	6.01	3.61	12.54	7.19	14.06	46.82	1.14	2.37	5.71	6.56	Ground corn and oats, weed seeds.
1933a	....do	13.34	2.67	10.28	5.38	9.65	45.65	.50	1.69	4.26	6.58	3.08	11.86	6.21	11.14	52.68	.58	1.95	4.92	7.59	Ground corn and oats.
	Average	10.83	2.99	10.89	5.99	11.27	44.29	.77	1.93	4.74	6.30	3.34	12.20	6.70	12.60	49.75	.86	2.16	5.32	7.07	
1958a	"0" white feed	11.54	2.81	10.17	4.90	10.34	45.39	1.21	1.12	4.12	8.40	3.17	11.49	5.54	11.70	51.32	1.37	1.27	4.65	9.49	Ground corn and oats, trace of rye, smartweed, and charlock.

a See page 71.

MIXED FEED.

Since the mixed feeds may, on account of their name, contain any mixture of ingredients that could be used as a cattle food, they can not be compared with standards. They can be compared with one another, however, and the microscopic examination shows what materials are present. It is evident from the results reported in Table 20 that this class of goods is made up principally of wheat products, varying from bran to Red Dog flour.

Nos. 1478 and 1825 are shown by the microscopical examination to contain corncobs and a wheat product. That some such substance has been added is also shown by the fact that the protein and fat content of these samples are markedly lower and the crude fiber content much higher than in the other mixed feeds.

The analysis of sample No. 1576 indicates that it is different from the other mixed feeds. That such is the case is shown by the microscopical examination of ground corn and oats and barley, as well as a small amount of a wheat product being present. The analysis of No. 1584 does not indicate that it is different from the other mixed feeds examined, except perhaps the starch figure is considerably above the average. The microscopical examination, however, shows this sample to be composed of a mixture of corn, oats, a wheat product, and small amounts of cottonseed and linseed meals.

TABLE 20.— *Mixed feed (percentage composition).*

Serial No.	Name and brand.	Moisture.	Calculated to basis of original sample.									Calculated to a moisture-free basis.									Raw materials identified by microscopical examination.
			Ash.	Crude protein.	Crude fiber.	Pentosan.	Starch.	Sucrose.	Reducing sugars.	Ether extract.	Undetermined.	Ash.	Crude protein.	Crude fiber.	Pentosan.	Starch.	Sucrose.	Reducing sugars.	Ether extract.	Undetermined.	
1473a	Med feed	8.36	5.48	17.00	8.96	21.93	18.79	4.84	1.58	5.10	7.96	5.98	18.56	9.78	23.93	20.50	5.28	1.72	5.57	8.68	W. P. No. 1, smartweed seed.
1779a	.....do	8.61	5.53	17.06	8.63	21.61	21.94	4.56	1.95	4.85	5.26	6.05	18.67	9.44	23.64	24.02	4.99	2.13	5.31	5.75	W. P. No.1, corn cockle and smartweed seed.
	Average	8.49	5.50	17.03	8.80	21.77	20.36	4.70	1.76	4.98	6.61	6.01	18.62	9.61	23.79	22.26	5.13	1.92	5.44	7.22	
1478a	Mixed feed, Blue Grass	8.16	3.40	10.00	17.50	25.12	18.75	2.22	1.42	2.26	11.17	3.70	10.89	19.05	27.35	20.42	2.42	1.55	2.46	12.16	W. P. No. 1, ground corncobs.
1497	Med feed	9.15	5.83	17.13	7.89	21.53	19.27	3.99	1.05	4.71	9.45	6.42	18.86	8.68	23.70	21.22	4.39	1.15	5.18	10.40	W. P. No.1.
1567	Med feed, Vermont	8.51	5.45	17.88	7.29	17.07	27.84	5.06	2.29	5.01	3.00	5.96	19.54	7.97	18.66	30.44	5.53	2.50	5.47	3.93	W. P. Nos. 1 and 2, corn cockle, smartweed.
1733	.....do	9.59	5.46	17.63	7.20	19.01	22.87	3.89	2.99	3.93	7.43	6.04	19.50	7.96	21.03	25.29	4.30	3.31	4.35	8.22	W. P. Nos. 1 and 2, smartweed.
1975	.....do	11.78	5.11	17.37	6.89	16.89	27.02	2.72	3.50	3.24	5.48	5.79	19.69	7.81	19.15	30.64	3.08	3.96	3.67	6.21	W. P. Nos. 1 and 2, corn cockle, pigweed, and smartweed.
	Average	9.96	5.34	17.63	7.13	17.65	25.91	3.89	2.93	4.06	5.505	5.93	19.58	7.91	19.61	28.79	4.30	3.26	4.50	6.12	
1483c	Med feed, Royal	9.13	5.11	16.75	7.88	19.06	24.94	3.90	1.48	4.66	7.09	5.62	18.43	8.67	20.97	27.46	4.29	1.63	5.13	7.80	W. P. No. 1, corn cockle, charlock.
1509c	Mixed feed, Stott's Honest	8.97	4.99	14.98	7.58	20.01	25.10	3.48	2.08	4.42	8.39	5.48	16.46	8.33	21.98	27.57	3.82	2.28	4.86	9.22	W. P. No. 1, chess, trace corn cockle, smartweed.
1980c	.....do	13.57	4.77	14.66	7.01	16.85	27.02	3.51	1.61	3.53	7.47	5.52	16.96	8.11	19.50	31.26	4.06	1.86	4.09	8.64	W. P. No. 1 and 2, trace corn cockle, smartweed.
	Average	11.27	4.88	14.82	7.30	18.43	26.06	3.49	1.84	3.98	7.93	5.50	16.71	8.22	20.74	29.42	3.94	2.07	4.47	8.93	
1525	Mixed feed	8.43	6.15	16.56	9.49	23.72	25.22	4.17	1.62	4.54	.10	6.72	18.08	10.36	25.90	27.50	4.56	1.81	4.96	.11	W. P. No. 1, trace of smartweed.
1597d	Mixed feed, flake	8.62	5.67	15.38	7.49	20.61	24.56	2.99	1.75	4.23	8.70	6.20	16.83	8.19	22.55	26.91	3.27	1.91	4.62	9.52	W. P. No. 2.
1602	Med feed	8.12	6.41	17.50	8.25	20.42	20.17	4.49	1.82	4.51	8.31	6.98	19.05	8.98	22.22	21.95	4.89	1.98	4.91	9.04	W. P. No.1.
1605	.....do	9.21	4.77	14.94	6.11	16.75	38.90	1.04	1.25	4.22	2.81	5.25	16.45	6.73	18.45	42.87	1.14	1.37	4.65	3.09	W. P. Nos. 1 and 2, trace of corn cockle.
1623	.....do	8.71	5.52	16.81	8.09	18.72	26.39	3.47	1.46	4.52	6.31	6.05	18.41	8.86	20.51	28.91	3.80	1.60	4.95	6.91	W. P. Nos. 1 and 2, smartweed, charlock.
1629	Mixed feed, Erie	9.12	6.03	15.88	8.03	20.05	19.82	4.68	1.74	4.09	10.56	6.64	17.47	8.84	22.04	21.83	5.15	1.91	4.50	11.62	W. P. Nos. 1 and 2, chess.
1694	Mixed feed, Monogram	8.74	5.45	17.31	7.05	19.04	26.81	4.67	2.14	4.89	3.90	5.97	18.97	7.73	20.86	29.38	5.12	2.34	5.36	4.27	W. P. Nos. 1, 2, and 3, corn cockle.
1867	Mixed feed, Occident	11.86	4.53	16.46	7.94	26.93	14.36	4.44	2.05	4.40	7.03	5.14	18.68	9.01	30.54	16.30	5.04	2.32	5.00	7.97	W. P. No. 1, smartweed.

No.	Name																				Remarks
1717	Mixed feed, Sunshine	8.62	5.36	17.75	7.42	18.65	27.09	4.88	1.08	4.15	5.00	5.86	19.42	8.12	20.41	29.66	5.34	1.18	4.54	5.47	W. P. Nos. 1 and 2, trace of corn cockle.
1721	Mixed feed, Boston	7.56	5.09	17.31	8.28	19.17	31.31	3.90	2.49	4.85	.04	5.51	18.72	8.96	20.74	33.88	4.22	2.69	5.24	.04	W. P. Nos. 1 and 2, corn cockle, smartweed.
1959	...do...	12.37	4.88	16.00	8.45	19.57	23.38	2.72	2.43	3.67	6.51	5.57	18.26	9.65	22.33	26.69	3.11	2.77	4.19	7.43	W. P. No. 1.
	Average	9.97	4.98	16.66	8.37	19.37	27.35	3.31	2.46	4.26	3.27	5.54	18.49	9.31	21.54	30.29	3.66	2.73	4.71	3.73	
1724	Mixed feed, Gold Mine	9.09	5.25	17.00	6.65	17.67	28.59	3.45	2.93	4.37	5.00	5.77	18.70	7.31	19.44	31.47	3.79	3.22	4.81	5.49	W. P. No. 1 and some No. 3, corn cockle.
1850	...do...	11.75	5.39	17.41	6.53	17.55	21.54	3.42	1.85	4.10	10.45	6.11	19.73	7.40	19.89	24.40	3.88	2.10	4.65	11.84	Do.
1755	Mixed feed	9.68	6.06	16.38	7.56	19.12	24.28	3.94	1.54	3.87	7.57	6.71	18.14	8.37	21.17	26.89	3.36	1.70	4.28	8.38	W. P. Nos. 1 and 2.
1780	...do...	7.76	5.89	15.88	7.75	20.35	28.59	4.48	1.57	4.30	3.43	6.38	17.21	8.40	22.08	30.99	4.86	1.70	4.66	3.72	W. P. No. 1, chess and corn cockle.
1787	Mixed feed, Superior	9.48	5.56	17.06	8.51	33.30	12.94	4.44	1.98	4.21	2.52	6.14	18.85	9.40	36.80	14.29	4.90	2.19	4.65	2.78	W. P. No. 1, corn cockle, smartweed.
1825	Mixed feed, Mascot	11.75	3.69	9.91	15.92	24.95	17.41	1.77	1.49	1.84	11.27	4.18	11.23	18.04	28.28	19.72	2.01	1.69	2.08	12.77	W. P. No. 2, ground corn-cob.
1827	Mixed feed, Crosby's Fancy	11.34	4.91	17.46	7.15	18.10	22.24	3.75	2.29	3.74	9.02	5.53	19.70	8.07	20.41	25.08	4.23	2.58	4.22	10.18	W. P. Nos. 1, 2, and 3.
1887	Mixed feed	13.46	5.22	14.01	6.38	17.14	26.73	4.19	1.24	3.61	8.02	6.03	16.18	7.38	19.80	30.90	4.84	1.43	4.17	9.27	W. P. Nos. 1 and 2.
1576	Mixed feed, C. & W	9.23	3.19	10.38	7.35	13.90	46.03	.84	1.52	2.21	5.35	3.51	11.44	8.10	15.32	50.72	.92	1.67	2.43	5.89	Ground corn and oats, small amount of barley and W. P. No. 2, weed seed.
1584	Mixed feed	8.48	3.56	15.75	6.44	12.02	44.25	1.47	1.63	4.72	1.68	3.89	17.21	7.03	13.13	48.36	1.61	1.78	5.16	1.83	Ground corn and oats, W. P. No. 2, small amount cottonseed meal, linseed meal.
1919	Mixed feed, Golden Bull	12.66	6.01	16.32	7.81	19.92	19.87	3.78	1.83	3.68	8.12	6.88	18.69	8.94	22.81	22.75	4.33	2.09	4.21	9.29	W. P. No. 1.
1926	Mixed feed, High Grade	12.08	5.96	17.19	7.87	18.15	21.69	2.73	2.29	3.65	8.39	6.78	19.55	8.95	20.64	24.68	3.10	2.61	4.15	9.54	W. P. Nos. 1, 2, and 3.
1955	Mixed feed, Duchess	13.11	2.36	15.14	9.83	18.26	25.64	2.52	2.47	3.56	7.11	2.72	17.41	11.32	21.01	29.51	2.90	2.85	4.10	8.18	W. P. No. 1 and small amount W. P. No. 3, smartweed seed.
1960	Mixed feed, Equality	14.49	3.92	16.42	8.07	17.75	26.13	2.37	2.00	3.04	5.81	4.58	19.20	9.44	20.76	30.55	2.78	2.34	3.56	6.79	W. P. No. 3.
1543	Tri-Me mixed feed	7.79	6.29	16.06	8.14	21.03	26.00	.96	.25	4.59	8.89	6.81	17.42	8.82	22.81	28.20	1.04	.27	4.98	9.64	W. P. No. 1, chess, yellow-dock seed.
1501	...do...	5.00	5.99	18.25	7.89	20.73	21.45	3.85	1.67	4.31	10.88	6.31	19.21	8.28	21.82	22.58	4.05	1.77	4.54	11.44	W. P. No. 1, smartweed seed.

a See page 70. b See page 63. c See page 69. d See page 67.

Only two samples of dried pulp were examined, neither of which shows adulteration. (Table 22.) The two samples labeled molasses feed evidently consist of a mixture of molasses and brewers' grains. Sample No. 1540 consists principally of a mixture of brewers' grains and molasses, with a small amount of linseed meal. Sample No. 1728 consists of a mixture of brewers' grains and molasses only. There is no feature of any of these analyses that would suggest adulteration.

MISCELLANEOUS FEEDS.

Under this heading are included a number of feeds which might, from their name, contain any mixture of ingredients or which have not been examined in large enough numbers to require a separate heading. The composition and ingredients of most of these are so plainly indicated by the chemical and microscopical examinations that separate mention of particular samples does not seem necessary, except in three cases.

Jenkins and Winton [a] give the following average composition for barley meal and screenings:

TABLE 21.—*Average percentage composition of barley meal and screenings.*

[Compiled.]

Constituents.	Number of analyses.	Moisture.	Ash.	Protein.	Crude fiber.	Nitrogen-free extract.	Fat.
Barley meal..................	3	11.9	2.6	10.5	6.5	66.3	2.2
Barley screenings............	2	12.2	3.6	12.3	7.3	61.8	2.8

It is evident that the two samples of barley meal examined, Nos. 1539 and 1698 (Table 23), compare favorably with the compiled results. Sample 1854, while having a high ash and fiber content, also contains a considerable amount of protein.

[a] Loc. cit.

TABLE 22.—*Sugar and molasses feeds.*

Serial No.	Name and brand.	Moisture.	Calculated to basis of original sample.									Calculated to a moisture-free basis.									Raw materials identified by microscopical examination.
			Ash.	Crude protein.	Crude fiber.	Pentosan.	Starch.	Sucrose.	Reducing sugars.	Ether extract.	Undetermined.	Ash.	Crude protein.	Crude fiber.	Pentosan.	Starch.	Sucrose.	Reducing sugars.	Ether extract.	Undetermined.	
1481	Dried beet pulp...	8.58	5.16	8.06	18.67	24.86	5.34	23.16	0.25	0.43	5.49	5.64	8.82	20.42	27.19	5.84	25.33	0.27	0.47	6.02	Dried beet pulp.
1829	....do.......	9.05	7.28	9.57	13.21	19.49	6.57	21.64	.51	.47	12.21	8.02	10.52	14.50	21.42	7.22	23.81	.57	.52	13.42	Do.
	Average.....	8.82	6.22	8.81	15.94	22.18	5.95	22.40	.38	.45	8.85	6.83	9.67	17.46	24.31	6.53	24.57	.42	.49	9.72	
1485	Molasses feed.....	7.66	5.95	23.88	11.22	15.26	14.50	6.43	9.85	4.40	.85	6.44	25.86	12.15	16.53	15.70	6.96	10.67	4.76	.93	Brewers' grains (barley hulls and sprouts).
1610	...do.....	11.71	6.72	20.31	9.94	12.89	12.22	16.47	6.35	1.97	1.42	7.61	23.01	11.26	14.60	13.84	18.65	7.19	2.23	1.61	Brewers' grains (barley).
1540	Molasses grains.....	7.05	7.53	16.94	10.88	14.48	7.97	13.89	8.42	3.08	9.76	8.08	18.25	11.71	15.58	8.57	14.94	9.06	3.31	10.50	Brewers' grains, largely oat hulls; barley hulls, linseed meal, smartweed, pigweed.
1728	.....do........	9.35	6.60	21.06	9.57	13.48	6.65	8.98	11.88	2.68	9.75	7.28	23.25	10.56	14.87	7.33	9.91	13.10	2.95	10.75	Brewers' grains, trace of oats.

TABLE 23.—*Miscellaneous feeds.*

Serial No.	Kind and brand.	Moisture.	\multicolumn{9}{Calculated to basis of original sample.}									\multicolumn{9}{Calculated to a moisture-free basis.}									Raw materials identified by microscopical examination.
			Ash.	Crude protein.	Crude fiber.	Pentosan.	Starch.	Sucrose.	Reducing sugars.	Ether extract.	Undetermined.	Ash.	Crude protein.	Crude fiber.	Pentosan.	Starch.	Sucrose.	Reducing sugars.	Ether extract.	Undetermined.	
1484	Salmon feed	10.97	2.31	7.63	8.23	14.94	42.05	1.18	0.96	2.74	8.99	2.59	8.53	9.24	16.78	47.28	1.32	1.08	3.08	10.10	Ground corn, barley, and small amount of oats.
1500	Ground feed	9.02	2.29	12.63	7.08	12.97	42.42	1.45	1.82	2.80	7.52	2.52	13.88	7.78	14.26	46.63	1.59	2.00	3.08	8.26	G md corn and oats, W. P. No. 3.
1536	...do...	7.67	6.75	13.19	12.23	17.59	31.12	2.02	2.20	2.98	4.25	7.31	14.29	13.25	19.05	33.70	2.19	2.38	3.23	4.60	Screenings, oats, W. P. No. 2, charlock, pigweed seed, 1 mustard.
1545	...do...	9.28	2.89	11.31	5.17	10.89	48.56	2.24	1.47	4.00	4.19	3.19	12.47	5.70	12.00	53.54	2.46	1.62	4.40	4.62	W. P. No. 1, cracked corn, whole oats, a trace of hay.
1551	Common feed	8.82	2.51	8.31	6.54	11.64	47.71	1.85	1.54	2.57	8.51	2.75	9.11	7.17	12.78	52.33	2.03	1.69	2.31	9.33	W. P. No. 1, gnd corn.
1571	Ground feed	8.71	3.88	10.13	6.21	10.42	45.58	1.41	2.17	2.91	8.58	4.25	11.10	6.80	11.41	49.93	1.54	2.38	3.19	9.40	gnd corn, oats, a wheat rpd... ut, and trace of gnd meal.
1609	Ground corn, oats, and rye.	9.15	6.07	10.06	7.17	10.35	51.65	1.04	1.39	2.91	.21	6.68	11.07	7.89	11.30	56.83	1.14	1.54	3.23	.23	G md corn, ats, orye, trace of oat, smartweed.
1627	Meal and shorts.	10.48	3.44	11.94	4.92	11.82	38.82	2.65	1.54	3.72	10.67	3.84	13.34	5.50	13.20	43.36	2.96	1.72	4.16	11.92	G md corn, W. P. No. 1.
1632	Felker's blended grain.	13.23	1.78	10.42	14.87	13.74	41.66	.59	1.51	1.95	.15	2.06	12.02	17.16	15.86	48.06	.68	1.75	2.25	.16	Cracked cn, whole wheat, barley, Kaffir corn, oats, smartweed seed.
1572a	M nh horse feed.	8.79	3.50	14.19	6.98	14.50	38.32	3.46	1.78	4.13	4.26	3.94	15.55	7.65	15.90	42.02	3.79	1.95	4.53	4.67	G md corn and oats, linseed meal, W. P. No. 2, and rye.
1539	Sper barley meal	8.11	3.86	14.13	7.16	13.55	42.84	1.47	2.42	2.99	3.47	4.20	15.38	7.79	14.75	46.62	1.60	2.63	3.25	3.78	G md barley.
1698	Barley ml.	9.13	4.93	14.00	9.68	15.43	29.65	2.60	1.38	3.76	9.44	5.43	15.41	10.65	16.98	32.62	2.86	1.52	4.14	10.39	Ground barley, with trace of oats.
1733	Rye mixed edd	7.30	4.81	16.25	5.03	19.45	28.09	5.46	1.23	3.14	9.24	5.18	17.53	5.43	20.98	30.30	5.89	1.33	3.39	9.97	W. P. No. 1, rye bran, trace of wild buckwheat, and smartweed.
1854b	clover meal.	7.05	19.74	17.19	18.81	8.14	14.81	0	1.48	3.22	9.56	21.26	18.49	20.23	8.76	15.93	0	1.59	3.46	10.28	Clover-seed chaff, plantain (*Plantago major*), and other weeds.

a See page 68.   *b* See page 65.

PROPRIETARY STOCK FEEDS.

Under this heading have been classified those feeds bearing trade names that are not descriptive in any way of the materials used. Like the miscellaneous feeds they may contain any mixture of stock food materials, and can not be compared with standards of average composition. The microscopic examination, however, shows plainly of what constituents these proprietary feeds are made. It will be noted that samples Nos. 1528 and 1700 contain corncob meal, and that several other samples contain considerable quantities of hulls. Samples Nos. 1575, 1726, and 1942, named sugar and flaxseed, are misbranded since the analyses and microscopical examination show other substances present than the ones mentioned in the name.

TABLE 24.—Proprietary stock feeds (percentage composition).

Serial No.	Name and brand.	Moisture.	Calculated to basis of original sample.									Calculated to a moisture-free basis.									Raw materials identified by microsopical examination.
			Ash.	Crude protein.	Crude fiber.	Pentosan.	Starch.	Sucrose.	Reducing sugars.	Ether extract.	Undetermined.	Ash.	Crude protein.	Crude fiber.	Pentosan.	Starch.	Sucrose.	Reducing sugars.	Ether extract.	Undetermined.	
1574	Schumacker's stock food.	7.24	4.79	11.38	11.71	17.66	28.31	1.74	2.17	5.50	9.50	5.16	12.27	12.62	19.04	30.53	1.87	2.34	5.93	10.24	Ground oats, W. P. No.1, corn meal.
1723	....do	7.60	4.91	12.12	10.01	15.64	31.78	2.15	3.01	4.14	8.64	5.31	13.12	10.83	16.93	34.39	2.33	3.26	4.48	9.35	Ground oats, corn meal, W. P. No. 1, foxtail seed, smartweed seed.
1928	....do	10.77	4.75	11.30	10.42	15.35	31.40	1.97	2.35	4.10	7.59	5.32	12.66	11.68	17.21	35.20	2.21	2.63	4.59	8.50	Ground oats, corn meal, W. P. No. 2, charlock.
	Average	8.54	4.82	11.60	10.71	16.22	30.49	1.95	2.51	4.58	8.58	5.26	12.68	11.71	17.76	33.37	2.13	2.74	5.00	9.35	
1590a	Blatchford's calf meal.	7.17	4.80	23.38	4.97	7.19	29.60	6.20	.48	4.43	11.78	5.17	25.19	5.35	7.74	31.88	6.68	.52	4.78	12.69	Linseed meal, cottonseed meal, some leguminous seeds, W. P. No. 3, carob bean and fenugrec.
1754c	....do	8.67	4.48	22.75	4.27	6.89	31.78	6.06	.66	4.38	10.06	4.90	24.91	4.68	7.54	34.81	6.64	.72	4.79	11.01	Linseed meal, cottonseed meal, W. P. No. 3, leguminous seeds, pigweed seed, carob bean and fenugrec.
	Average	7.92	4.64	23.07	4.62	7.04	30.69	6.13	.57	4.40	10.92	5.03	25.05	5.01	7.64	33.35	6.66	.62	4.79	11.85	
1757	H-O horse feed	8.36	3.53	11.69	9.30	14.10	38.34	1.39	1.85	3.47	7.39	3.85	12.76	10.15	16.02	41.84	1.52	2.02	3.78	8.06	Ground corn and oats, W. P. No. 2.
1988	....do	11.24	3.03	11.99	9.06	14.10	36.14	1.88	1.04	3.75	7.77	3.41	13.51	10.20	15.89	40.71	2.12	1.17	4.23	8.76	Do.
	Average	9.80	3.28	11.84	9.18	14.39	37.24	1.64	1.44	3.61	7.58	3.63	13.14	10.18	15.95	41.28	1.82	1.59	4.00	8.41	
1489	Merchant's dairy feed.	6.13	1.65	31.25	12.98	24.44	3.09	0	0	11.49	8.97	1.76	33.29	13.83	26.04	3.29	0	0	12.24	9.55	Distillers' dried grains (corn and barley).
1784	....do	6.37	1.99	30.19	13.53	24.23	4.59	0	0	11.37	7.73	2.12	32.26	14.45	25.88	4.90	0	0	12.14	8.25	Do.
	Average	6.25	1.82	30.72	13.25	24.34	3.84	0	0	11.43	8.35	1.94	32.78	14.14	25.96	4.09	0	0	12.19	8.90	
1528	Star feed	8.07	2.55	8.38	9.60	13.97	42.00	2.16	.44	5.92	6.91	2.77	9.11	10.44	15.20	45.69	2.35	.48	6.44	7.52	Corn and corncob meal.
1700	....do	8.61	2.53	8.94	7.42	13.94	43.50	1.99	.27	5.69	7.11	2.77	9.78	8.11	15.25	47.60	2.18	.30	6.23	7.78	Corn meal, some corncob.
	Average	8.34	2.54	8.66	8.51	13.96	42.75	2.07	.35	5.81	7.01	2.77	9.44	9.28	15.23	46.65	2.26	.39	6.33	7.65	
1615b	Empire feed	9.77	2.12	7.69	6.82	10.88	57.47	.95	.90	2.35	1.05	2.35	8.53	7.56	12.06	63.69	1.05	1.00	2.60	1.16	Ground corn and oats.
1753b	....do	23.12	1.87	6.46	7.65	8.38	44.66	.40	.52	1.07	5.87	2.44	8.40	9.94	10.90	58.10	.52	.67	1.39	7.64	Ground corn and oats, with possibly small excess of oat hulls, rough pigweed.
	Average	16.45	1.99	7.07	7.24	9.63	51.07	.67	.71	1.71	3.46	2.40	8.47	8.75	11.48	60.90	.78	.83	1.99	4.40	

No.	Feed																				Composition
1583c	Buffalo horse feed	8.55	3.40	12.25	10.32	15.78	33.38	1.81	1.95	4.93	7.63	3.72	13.40	11.28	17.26	36.51	1.97	2.13	5.39	8.34	Corn meal, ground oats, W. P. No. 2, linseed meal, trace of corn cockle.
1954c	...do	10.82	3.12	11.06	10.49	15.19	35.39	1.31	2.37	3.30	6.95	3.50	12.40	11.76	17.03	39.69	1.47	2.66	3.70	7.79	Corn meal, ground oats, linseed meal, W. P. No.1.
	Average	9.68	3.26	11.65	10.41	15.49	34.39	1.56	2.16	4.12	7.29	3.61	12.90	11.52	17.15	38.10	1.72	2.39	4.54	8.07	
1523c	Buffalo creamery feed	7.09	4.05	18.56	11.70	16.70	28.80	1.86	1.88	5.47	3.89	4.36	19.98	12.59	17.98	31.00	2.00	2.02	5.89	4.18	Corn meal, ground oats, W. P. Nos. 1 or 2, cottonseed meal.
1541c	...do	6.85	3.99	19.81	9.88	16.50	28.44	1.77	.26	5.14	7.66	4.28	21.27	10.61	17.71	30.22	1.90	.28	5.51	8.22	Corn meal, ground oats, cottonseed meal, rough pigweed seed.
1972c	...do	9.81	3.68	18.06	11.78	17.14	26.12	2.25	1.00	3.81	6.35	4.08	20.03	13.06	19.01	28.97	2.49	1.11	4.22	7.04	Corn meal, ground oats, W. P. Nos. 1 and 2, cottonseed meal.
	Average	7.92	3.91	18.81	11.12	16.78	27.69	1.96	1.05	4.81	5.97	4.24	20.43	12.09	18.23	30.06	2.13	1.14	5.21	6.48	
1573c	B llo dairy fd	7.09	3.43	12.69	13.56	20.36	28.87	1.19	1.63	3.49	7.69	3.69	13.66	14.59	21.91	31.08	1.28	1.75	3.76	8.28	Orn ml, ground oats, W. P. No.2.
1476	Great orn dairy fd	7.49	5.50	8.06	20.60	23.47	24.28	.65	1.03	1.92	7.00	5.95	8.71	22.27	25.37	26.25	.70	1.11	2.07	7.57	Ground oats and oat ulls, corn ml.
1488	P rn ground fd	7.87	3.92	7.56	15.04	18.74	40.50	.58	.59	2.43	2.77	4.25	8.20	16.32	20.34	43.97	.63	.64	2.64	3.01	G und oats and corn, oat ulls hi—lly
1503	Empire ste dairy feed	4.99	1.98	30.06	12.86	20.60	15.23	0	.56	10.89	2.83	2.08	31.66	13.52	21.68	16.03	0	.59	11.46	2.98	Principally corn and barley hi—probably a brewery or lly pt.
1506	B mo feed	10.68	8.63	14.94	13.14	13.00	17.25	2.70	12.50	.87	6.29	9.66	16.72	14.71	14.55	19.34	3.02	13.99	.97	7.04	Oat hulls and brewery grains, and tall grass.
1550	Lenox sok fd	7.66	2.95	7.38	12.09	17.36	46.97	.88	1.09	3.23	.39	3.19	7.99	13.09	18.80	50.88	.95	1.18	3.50	.42	Orn and oat ml. and, and orn
1611	Boston feed	8.77	5.24	16.69	8.64	20.08	29.44	4.35	1.72	4.57	.50	5.74	18.29	9.47	22.01	32.28	4.77	1.88	5.01	.55	W. P. No.1, hle seed.
1613	Mel fd	9.32	6.07	16.99	8.30	21.26	19.57	4.62	1.31	4.04	8.82	6.09	18.41	9.15	23.45	21.58	5.09	1.44	4.46	9.73	W. P. No.1, ard 2, seed of broad-
1716	Delaware fd	8.75	5.52	15.75	7.76	19.32	30.65	5.78	.82	4.23	1.42	6.05	17.26	8.50	21.17	33.61	6.33	.90	4.63	1.55	W. P. Nos.1 and dk, orn okle.
1729	Manna ml e and fd	18.88	2.35	6.72	9.47	12.13	43.03	.53	.81	2.02	4.06	2.90	8.28	11.68	14.94	53.04	.66	1.00	2.49	5.01	Corn and oat meal.
1743	King feed	8.70	6.24	17.00	8.09	18.68	24.28	4.92	1.36	4.09	6.64	6.83	18.62	8.86	20.46	26.60	5.39	1.49	4.48	7.27	W. P. No. 1, chess and smartweed seed.
1824	Rd he fd	13.31	2.24	9.45	4.52	25.16	39.32	.68	1.02	3.38	.92	2.59	10.89	5.21	29.02	45.35	.79	1.18	3.90	1.06	Corn and oat meal.
1831	ll's sok fod	9.85	2.91	8.95	6.88	11.03	45.40	2.04	.45	4.86	7.63	3.23	9.93	7.63	12.24	50.36	2.26	1.50	5.39	8.46	Corn meal with some oat meal.
1575c	Blatchford's spar and fd	7.76	5.23	27.13	6.69	7.61	12.15	7.16	.62	10.24	15.41	5.67	29.42	7.25	8.25	13.17	7.76	0.67	6.71	16.71	Linseed meal, cottonseed meal, leguminous seed, W. P. No.3, carob bean, trace of fenugree and anise seed.
1726	...do	7.28	5.17	28.25	5.85	6.86	12.09	6.75	.67	10.78	16.30	5.57	30.48	6.31	7.40	13.04	7.28	.72	11.62	17.58	Linseed meal, cottonseed meal, leguminous seed, W. P. No. 3, carob bean, fenugree.
1942	...do	13.23	5.17	26.64	5.41	7.57	11.39	6.81	.75	9.74	13.29	5.96	30.69	6.24	8.72	13.13	7.85	.86	11.23	15.32	Linseed meal, cottonseed meal, leguminous seed, trace of pigweed seed, carob bean, fenugree. W. P. No.3.
	Average	9.42	5.19	27.34	5.98	7.35	11.88	6.91	.68	10.25	15.00	5.73	30.20	6.60	8.12	13.11	7.63	.75	11.32	16.54	

ANIMAL MEALS.

Under this head are included meat, meat and bone, bone, and blood meals. All the samples examined were of satisfactory composition. Their high protein content makes them valuable in remedying the deficiency of this essential constituent in the so-called "carbohydrate feeds." Bowker's animal meal contains considerable cottonseed meal, as shown by both the microscopical and chemical examination.

TABLE 25.—*Animal meals (percentage composition).*

Serial No.	Name and brand.	Moisture.	Calculated to basis of original sample.									Calculated to a moisture-free basis.									Raw materials identified by microscopical examination.
			Ash.	Crude protein.	Crude fiber.	Pentosan.	Starch.	Sucrose.	Reducing sugars.	Ether extract.	Undetermined.	Ash.	Crude protein.	Crude fiber.	Pentosan.	Starch.	Sucrose.	Reducing sugars.	Ether extract.	Undetermined.	
1557	Bowker's animal meal.	6.08	38.32	34.69	4.26	1.81	0	1.67	0	9.87	3.30	40.80	36.95	4.54	1.91	0	1.77	0	10.50	3.53	Animal meal, bone, and cotton-seed meal.
1744	...do...	5.29	29.21	40.88	4.32	3.07	0	1.82	0	8.32	7.09	30.84	43.18	4.56	3.24	0	1.89	0	8.78	7.51	Do.
	Average.	5.68	33.77	37.79	4.29	2.44	0	1.74	0	9.09	5.20	35.82	40.07	4.55	2.57	0	1.83	0	9.64	5.52	
1737	Granulated poultry bone.	6.39	60.94	25.75						1.47	5.45	65.10	27.51						1.57	5.82	Ground bone.
1748	Coarse poultry bone.	6.59	65.76	23.44						.69	3.52	70.41	25.09						.73	3.77	Coarsely-cracked bone.
1822	Marsh's pure bone meal.	8.97	68.76	15.46						4.54	2.27	75.54	16.99						4.98	2.49	Finely ground bone meal.
1900	Bone meal.	9.67	60.14	25.36						1.47	3.26	66.69	28.08						1.63	3.60	Do.
1931	Cut green bone.	9.68	59.47	27.60						1.15	2.10	65.85	30.55						1.28	2.32	Bone meal.
1696	Blood meal.	7.98	3.88	85.81						.24	2.09	4.22	93.25						.26	2.25	Dried blood.
1732	Armour's pure blood meal.	8.65	2.49	87.31						.12	1.43	2.72	95.59						.13	1.56	Do.
1965	...do...	10.53	3.81	84.54						.13	.99	4.25	94.50						.15	1.10	Do.
	Average.	9.59	3.15	85.93						.12	1.21	3.48	95.05						.14	1.33	
1773a	Swift's blood meal.	7.72	3.89	85.56						.28	2.55	4.21	92.73						.30	2.76	Do.

a See page 70.

POULTRY FOODS.

It would appear from the microscopical examination of this class of goods that most of them are composed largely of screenings from various grains, or of very inferior grains. Many varieties of weed seeds are present, but in only one case is there enough of a poisonous weed seed to make the use of the food objectionable. This, is sample No. 1556, which contains a considerable quantity of darnel (*Lolium temulentum*), a weed seed with marked toxic properties. While the chemical composition of most of these foods shows them to have considerable food value, yet many of them are sold under names which are misleading. Such names as "Laying food," "Egg-builder ration," and "Forcing food," at least imply that the foods in question have certain egg forcing properties in addition to their ordinary food value. Such is not the case, however, the foods' only increasing the amount of laying by supplying to the hen those food constituents which keep her in first class physical condition and which are needed to build up the egg and shell. Since protein is one of the constituents usually lacking in the food ordinarily fed to chickens, and since also it forms a large portion of the egg, the foods which contain this constituent in large amounts are generally to be preferred.

TABLE 26.—Poultry foods (percentage composition).

Serial No.	Name and brand.	Moisture.	Calculated to basis of original sample.									Calculated to a moisture-free basis.									Raw materials identified by microscopical examination.
			Ash.	Crude protein.	Crude fiber.	Pentosan.	Starch.	Sucrose.	Reducing sugars.	Ether extract.	Undetermined.	Ash.	Crude protein.	Crude fiber.	Pentosan.	Starch.	Sucrose.	Reducing sugars.	Ether extract.	Undetermined.	
1521a	Puritan chick food	8.32	6.13	12.25	5.54	11.37	35.34	2.77	1.34	6.80	10.14	6.68	13.36	6.04	12.40	38.56	3.02	1.46	7.42	11.06	Corn meal, W. P. No. 2, trace of oats and animal meal.
1529	H-O poultry food	8.38	2.67	16.13	4.62	11.33	37.78	2.43	1.47	5.58	9.61	2.91	17.61	5.04	12.37	41.24	2.65	1.60	6.09	10.49	Corn meal, W. P. No. 1, rolled oats and small amount of peanut.
1776	...do...	7.97	2.97	18.13	5.54	13.83	36.65	1.49	1.07	5.45	6.90	3.23	19.70	6.02	15.03	39.83	1.62	1.16	5.92	7.50	Corn meal, W. P. No. 1, rolled oats; trace of corn cockle.
	Average	8.18	2.82	17.13	5.08	12.58	37.22	1.96	1.27	5.51	8.26	3.07	18.66	5.53	13.70	40.54	2.14	1.38	6.00	9.00	
1532	American poultry food	8.68	3.27	13.69	4.65	11.55	38.56	2.93	1.29	9.85	5.53	3.58	14.99	5.09	12.65	42.22	3.21	1.41	16.79	6.06	Corn meal, W. P. Nos. 1 and 2.
1581b	Cypher's laying food	9.83	5.12	15.94	5.43	10.06	42.47	2.22	1.31	3.65	3.94	5.68	17.69	6.02	11.16	47.11	2.46	1.45	4.05	4.38	W. P. No. 1, corn meal and some animal meal.
1795b	...do...	9.66	5.32	15.50	4.65	6.36	48.28	.87	1.46	2.03	5.85	5.89	17.16	5.15	7.04	53.45	.96	1.62	2.25	6.48	W. P. No. 1, corn meal, animal meal, seeds of smart weed, foxtail grass, and charlock.
1893b	...do...	14.84	5.14	15.04	7.30	4.65	40.69	.98	1.19	3.01	7.16	5.03	17.66	8.57	5.46	47.78	1.16	1.40	3.53	8.41	W. P. No. 1, corn meal and animal meal.
	Average	11.45	5.19	15.50	5.79	7.02	43.82	1.36	1.32	2.90	5.65	5.87	17.50	6.58	7.89	49.44	1.53	1.49	3.28	6.42	
1556a	Egg builder ration	8.29	16.20	12.75	4.15	5.25	41.76	.29	.98	3.54	6.79	17.67	13.90	4.52	5.72	45.54	.32	1.07	3.86	7.40	Kaffir corn, wheat, stone, cracked corn, ground bone, buckwheat, millet, foxtail grass, charcoal, flaxseed, sunflower, oats, rye, charlock, rose seed, Lolium temulentum.
1582c	Poultry feed	8.48	2.91	15.56	4.78	10.08	36.15	2.01	1.26	8.23	10.54	3.18	17.00	5.22	11.01	39.51	2.20	1.38	8.99	11.51	Cracked corn, ground oats, W. P. No. 1, trace of charlock seed.
1683b	Cypher's scratching food	8.32	5.79	15.94	7.48	8.30	37.00	4.60	1.78	4.51	6.28	6.32	17.39	8.16	9.05	40.34	5.02	1.94	4.93	6.85	W. P. No. 2.
1711a	Unexcelled baby chick food.	9.15	8.84	11.38	3.77	4.37	47.44	1.16	.87	4.44	8.58	9.73	12.53	4.15	4.80	52.24	1.28	.95	4.88	9.44	Cracked corn, millet, foxtail, cracked wheat, pigweed seed, corn cockle, flaxseed, Kaffir corn, Brassica (sp.) ground rock, charcoal.

a See page 66.   b See page 65.   c See page 63.

TABLE 26.—*Poultry foods (percentage composition)*—Continued.

Serial No.	Brand.	Calculated to basis of original sample.										Calculated to a moisture-free basis.									Raw materials identified by microscopical examination.
		Moisture.	Ash.	Crude protein.	Crude fiber.	Pentosan.	Starch.	Sucrose.	Reducing sugars.	Ether extract.	Undetermined.	Ash.	Crude protein.	Crude fiber.	Pentosan.	Starch.	Sucrose.	Reducing sugars.	Ether extract.	Undetermined.	
1930a	Unexcelled baby chick food.	10.20	11.74	11.37	4.98	4.97	44.65	1.40	1.31	3.41	5.97	13.07	12.66	5.55	5.54	49.73	1.56	1.45	3.79	6.65	Cracked corn, millet, foxtail, wheat screenings, Kaffir corn, smartweed, ground rock, charlock, oats, pigweed seed, charcoal, flaxseed, pigeon grass.
	Average..........	9.68	10.29	11.38	4.37	4.67	46.05	1.28	1.09	3.92	7.27	11.40	12.59	4.85	5.17	50.99	1.42	1.20	4.34	8.05	
1738a	Blatchford's poultry meats.	6.21	23.65	31.50	7.04	1.88	13.22	0	0	7.32	9.18	25.23	33.59	7.50	2.00	14.09	0	0	7.80	9.79	Ground bone, animal meal, linseed meal, cottonseed meal, some W. P., sunflower seeds, oyster shells, trace of capsicum.
1739c	Chick food..........	8.37	12.56	11.38	4.65	5.33	46.65	.63	1.23	2.44	6.74	13.71	12.42	5.07	5.82	50.95	.69	1.34	2.66	7.34	Mostly wheat screenings with millet, foxtail, charlock, smartweed, corn, linseed, oats, rock, chess, rough pigweed.
1759c	Forcing food..........	9.13	5.87	15.56	5.03	9.14	45.19	1.54	1.80	2.67	3.07	6.46	17.11	5.54	10.06	49.74	1.69	1.98	4.04	3.38	Corn meal, W. P. No. 1, smartweed, leguminous seed, some animal meal, wheat screenings.
1794	ard Peep 'Day chick food.	9.16	10.04	11.56	3.75	4.42	50.90	.92	1.33	3.85	4.07	11.05	12.72	4.13	4.86	56.05	1.01	1.46	4.24	4.48	Cracked corn, millet, Kaffir corn, smartweed, wheat, flaxseed, black oats, Brassica (sp.), pigweed seed, charcoal, quartz rock.
1814	Nursery chick food, No.1	7.82	16.25	16.58	14.33	12.19	24.81	2.29	1.93	3.45	.34	17.63	17.99	15.55	13.23	26.93	2.49	2.10	3.74	.34	W. P. No. 1, oats without hulls and small amt of corn.
1815	Growing chick food, No.2	8.66	15.45	20.16	6.24	11.51	23.80	1.76	1.61	2.45	8.34	16.91	22.07	6.83	12.60	26.09	1.93	1.76	2.68	9.13	W. P. No. 1 and oats with but few hulls.
1820d	Chick meal..........	9.29	8.66	21.18	1.21	2.31	44.54	2.26	1.67	2.93	5.95	9.55	23.35	1.33	2.55	49.10	2.49	1.84	3.23	6.56	Mly starchy, and oyster shells, charlock, out.
1826	Chick feed..........	10.16	15.40	10.30	3.94	6.05	39.48	1.36	3.76	2.24	7.31	17.14	11.46	4.39	6.73	43.95	1.51	4.18	2.50	8.14	Newwheat bit oat, corn, rolled oats, millet, flaxseed, coal, smartweed, yellow dock seed, ground rock, pigeon grass, pigweed seed, Stramonium.
1846	O. K. poultry meal......	12.43	5.76	15.57	4.95	8.47	38.84	2.01	1.66	3.46	6.85	6.58	17.77	5.65	9.67	44.37	2.29	1.90	3.95	7.82	W. P. No. 1 and wheat, and corn meal, animal meal, and trace of oats.

No.																			Description
1960a	Chicken wheat	10.68	11.67	12.70	6.62	7.22	37.46	1.38	1.92	9.10	13.06	14.22	7.41	8.08	41.95	1.55	2.14	1.40 10.19	Wheat screenings, chess, barley, rye, ground oyster shells, pepper grass, smartweed, green foxtail, pigweed.
1881	Chicken feed	11.59 12.17	9.85	4.57	2.15	48.19	1.05	.64	8.07 13.77	11.15	5.16	2.43	54.51	1.18	.73	1.95 9.12			Millet, hulled oats, cracked wheat, cracked corn, pigeon grass, foxtail, Kaffir corn, trace of charcoal, ground bone, linseed, rock.
1903	Poultry feed	10.81 3.53	16.79 10.69	13.29	31.95	2.67	2.02	4.40 3.96	18.82 11.99	14.91	35.81	2.99	2.27	4.32 4.93				Corn meal, oats, W. P. No. 1, trace of corn cockle.
1905	Egg and feather producing food, No. 4	9.38 15.62	21.46	5.97	3.22	33.93	1.71	2.04	4.52 17.24	23.68	6.59	3.55	37.44	1.88	2.26	2.37 4.99			W. P. No. 1, ground oats (very few hulls), and dried blood.
1906	Puritan laying stock food	10.91 6.06	12.37	5.92 22.81	32.87	2.07	1.97	.75 6.80	13.89	6.64	25.61	36.90	2.32	2.21	4.79 .84			Corn meal and oats, W. P. No. 2.
1915f	Perfect chick food	9.99 23.06	10.46	3.06	4.31	37.26	.56	.93	8.42 25.62	11.62	3.40	4.78	41.42	.62	1.03	2.16 9.35			Cracked wheat, cracked Kaffir corn, ground rock, oyster shells, millet, ground, legumins seed, husk, yellow dock, plantain.
1920e	Wyandotte chicken food	10.34 16.53	8.90	3.34	3.84	46.40	.64	.87	7.00 18.44	9.92	3.73	4.28	51.75	.72	.97	2.39 7.80			Cracked corn, oats, ground oyster shells, fine charcoal, trace of charlock, and smartweed.
1923d	Scratching feed	12.15 12.00	9.59	5.38	5.10	47.12	.96	1.99	4.39 13.66	10.92	6.12	5.81	53.63	1.09	2.26	1.51 5.00			Common millet, and broom corn variety, charcoal, rock, cracked wheat, cracked corn, smartweed.
1935	Poultry hash	11.53 5.33	14.53	7.90	12.10	31.02	2.18	2.69	9.41 6.04	16.43	8.94	13.68	35.02	2.45	3.05	3.74 10.65			W. P. No. 2, corn meal, oats, linseed meal.
1936	High-grade scratching feed	12.70 1.87	11.99	2.27	5.62	52.71	.90	1.96	8.02 2.15	13.93	2.60	6.44	60.37	1.03	2.25	2.25 9.18			Wheat, Kaffir corn, cracked corn, hulled oats, rye, traces of barley, smartweed, and flaxseed.
1940	Choice chicken feed	13.07 2.40	13.02	3.67	4.68	50.17	.85	1.53	8.15 2.76	14.98	4.22	5.38	57.73	.98	1.76	2.82 9.37			corn, millet, wheat screenings, Kaffir corn, trace of charcoal, smartweed, Convgia orientalis, corn cake, oats, foxtail.
1944	Webster's scratching feed	12.54 2.52	11.92	3.42	5.89	49.51	1.59	2.12	8.42 2.88	13.64	3.91	6.73	56.61	1.82	2.43	2.36 9.62			Cracked corn, wheat, millet, smartweed seed.
1946	O. K. poultry food	17.79 30.39	32.70	....	....	....	13.91	....	5.21 36.97	39.77	....	....	....	....	....	16.92 6.34			Mixture of bone meal.
1986	H-O pigeon feed	13.67 1.73	10.44	1.96	5.61	56.90	1.13	1.54	4.75 2.00	12.09	2.27	6.49	65.94	1.31	1.78	2.62 5.50			Wheat screenings, cracked corn, hulled oats, trace of rye, corn cockle, millet, peas, charlock.

a See page 66. b See page 61. c See page 65. d See page 68. e See page 69. f See page 64. g See page 63.

COMPARISON OF COMMERCIAL AND HOME-GROWN FEEDS.

A study of commercial feeding stuffs would not be complete without some mention of the relative feeding value and economy of such feeds as compared with those that can be grown on the farm. It is of course at times desirable or even necessary to use some of the more concentrated commercial feeds in the case of growing animals, in milk production, etc., but in the great majority of cases the cost of mixing such standard concentrated feeds as dried blood, cotton-seed meal, linseed meal, and brewery and distillery wastes with the products from the farm is much less when this work is performed by the farmer himself, rather than when it is performed by the manufacturer.

In the bulletin of Jenkins and Winton, previously quoted, it is shown that some of the more common farm crops used for feeding purposes have the average composition given in Table 27.

TABLE 27.—*Average percentage composition of home-grown feeds.*

Fodders.	Fresh, or air-dry, basis.						Calculated to dry basis.				
	Moisture.	Ash.	Protein.	Crude fiber.	Nitrogen-free extract.	Fat.	Ash.	Protein.	Crude fiber.	Nitrogen-free extract.	Fat.
Corn fodder—field-cured	42.2	2.7	4.5	14.3	34.7	1.6	4.7	7.8	24.7	60.1	2.8
Corn stover—field-cured	40.1	3.4	3.8	19.7	31.9	1.1	5.7	6.4	33.0	53.2	1.7
Red top hay	8.9	5.2	7.9	28.6	47.4	1.9	5.7	8.7	31.4	52.1	2.1
Timothy hay	13.2	4.4	5.9	29.0	45.0	2.5	5.1	6.8	33.5	51.7	2.9
Red clover hay	15.3	6.2	12.3	24.8	38.1	3.3	7.3	14.5	29.1	45.2	3.9
Alsike clover hay	9.7	8.3	12.8	25.6	40.7	2.9	9.3	14.2	28.4	44.9	3.2
White clover hay	9.7	8.3	15.7	24.1	39.3	2.9	9.2	17.4	26.7	43.5	3.2
Alfalfa hay	8.4	7.4	14.3	25.0	42.7	2.2	8.1	15.6	27.3	46.6	2.4
Corn—Dent	10.6	1.5	10.3	2.2	70.4	5.0	1.7	11.5	2.6	78.6	5.6
Corn—Flint	11.3	1.4	10.5	1.7	70.1	5.0	1.7	11.8	1.9	79.0	5.6
Oats	11.0	3.0	11.8	9.5	59.7	5.0	3.4	13.2	10.8	67.0	5.6
Barley	10.9	2.4	12.4	2.7	69.8	1.8	2.7	13.9	3.0	78.4	2.0
Rye	11.6	1.9	10.6	1.7	72.5	1.7	2.1	12.0	1.9	82.2	1.9
Cowpeas	14.8	3.2	20.8	4.1	55.7	1.4	3.8	24.4	4.8	65.5	1.7

These home-grown feeds could be better compared with the commercial feeds if the digestible nutrients in all of the latter were known, but since this is not the case, only a comparison of feeding values, based on the total nutrients present, can be made. It is not necessary to make this comparison in each individual case, but the general conclusion resulting from such a study would be that in a large number of cases the home-grown feeds are superior to the commercial feeds, especially in the case of those commercial feeding stuffs bearing a fancy name, which entirely masks the ingredients used. Furthermore, in many cases the commercial mixtures that do really have a higher nutritive value than the ordinary home-grown feeds could be much more economically prepared on the farm by buying the standard concentrated feeds, such as blood meal, cotton-seed and linseed meal, etc., and mixing them with home-grown crops.

CORRESPONDENCE WITH MANUFACTURERS.

In order that all manufacturers whose cattle foods were examined might have a chance to inspect the analyses before their publication and offer such explanations as they thought best of discrepancies between the guaranteed analysis and the analysis as found, also that they might explain any adulteration if such existed, the following circular letter was sent to every manufacturer whose goods were examined:

DEAR SIR: The miscellaneous laboratory of this Bureau, during the past two years, has been making chemical and microscopical analyses of the various commercial feeding stuffs sold on the American market, and will shortly publish the results of this work. The examination of ———— has given the following results:

Per cent.

Moisture	
Ash	
Ether extract (fat)	
Proteids	
Crude fiber	
Pentosans	
Starch	
Reducing sugars	
Sucrose	
Undetermined	
Total	

MICROSCOPICAL EXAMINATION.

We are sending to each manufacturer a copy of the analysis of his feeding stuff before publishing the results, that he may, if he so desires, explain any differences existing between the composition as determined by us and as claimed by him. If the analyses do differ materially, any legitimate explanation which the manufacturer makes will be carefully considered and published with the analysis of the feeding stuff.

If the manufacturer makes no claims in regard to the composition of his goods, the above remarks do not apply to him, and the data are sent only for his personal information. You, of course, understand that these results are not to be used for advertising purposes. A prompt reply will be appreciated.

Respectfully,

(Signed)   H. W. WILEY,
Chief of Bureau.

Following are such excerpts from the replies received as throw any light on the subject, together with the comments thereon made by the chemists who performed the work.

J. W. BARWELL.

(Nos. 1590, 1754, 1738, 1575, 1726, 1942.)

I am duly in receipt of your tabulated results of the examination of Blatchford's calf meal, Blatchford's poultry meats, and Blatchford's sugar and flaxseed.

I am inclined to think that some of these samples were taken some time ago, and do not represent the goods as now turned out, or as they have been turned out for the last eighteen months. The cause of the change was the necessary introduction of a specially prepared soluble blood flour into Blatchford's calf meal (Nos. 1590, 1754) in order to bring up the percentage of protein, as the more exhaustive machinery now used in the manufacture of some of the ingredients has reduced the amount of fat and protein in those ingredients.

In the results of your microscopical examination of Blatchford's calf meal, it states that middlings or shorts and pigweed are found, and I would say that I am prepared to go into any court of law and to put up any bond * * * that there are no wheat middlings or shorts or pigweed [used]. The pigweed, I take it, must have been some trifling weed seed that got into one of the ingredients * * *

In the results of the microscopical examination of Blatchford's sugar and flaxseed (Nos. 1575, 1726, 1942), the results might possibly lead people to suppose that there were only those articles or ingredients in our product that are mentioned by the microscopist, but this is not so. For instance, there are nine different ingredients in Blatchford's calf meal, but there are only three or four mentioned by the microscopist. There is considerable carob-bean meal used in both the calf meal and sugar and flaxseed, but this is not mentioned at all. There is considerable sunflower seed used in the manufacture of Blatchford's poultry meats, but this is not mentioned. * * *

Comment by authors.—The microscopical examination on all of Mr. Barwell's goods was repeated, and the manufacturer was informed that the samples were taken more than eighteen months ago.

In Blatchford's calf meal the microscopical finding of middlings was changed to flour. Several ingredients mentioned by the manufacturer were found and are given in the analysis as repeated. It was impossible, however, to find one or two condimental materials claimed by the manufacturer.

In Blatchford's sugar and flaxseed, carob-bean meal was found, as well as very small quantities of several other ingredients mentioned by the manufacturer. One or two condimental materials mentioned by the manufacturer could not be found.

In Blatchford's poultry meats sunflower seeds were found and several other ingredients that were present in very small quantities. It was impossible to find one or two condimental materials claimed by the manufacturer.

THE J. W. BILES' COMPANY.

(No. 1819.)

*. * * We beg to state, however, that your sample showed a rather unusually high per cent of water. * * * Protein and fat are each about one point lower than average, and the per cent of fiber is a little too high. * * * As to your microscopical analysis, we regret to say that it is essentially wrong and misleading, and this we must request you to change before your report is published. * * *

Union grains are made of—

(1) Fourex, which is a distiller's dried grain produced from the slop of spirits and grain alcohol distilleries.

(2) Choice cottonseed meal.

(3) Old process linseed meal.

(4) White wheat middlings.

(5) Wheat bran.

(6) Hominy meal.

(7) Barley malt sprouts, which contain some barley hulls and most always some weed seeds, though never in greater than entirely negligible quantities.

(8) Fine table salt, 1.5 per cent of the whole.

Comment by authors.—This sample was examined chemically a second time and the same results obtained as on the first examination. It was again examined by the microscopist and the results as given in the table were obtained.

(Nos. 1768, 1589, 1695, 1990.)

We have received your reports of 1768, rye distillers' dried grains, and 1589, 1695, and 1990, on the samples of Biles fourex distillers' dried grains. * * * There are a very large number of analyses of fourex and other distillers' dried grains on record in the six New England States and the State of New York, and if you will have these looked over you will find but very few analyses which show less than 11 per cent fat—the average is over 12 per cent. * * * We do not recollect having ever seen a report which showed less than 10 per cent fat. * * *

The microscopical analysis should show traces of oats, because all distillers use some oats, we think, but few use rye.

Comment by authors.—The results on fat were repeated and the same results obtained as previously. The microscopical analyses were repeated, and rye was again found, but no oats.

BOSWORTH & WOOD.

(No. 1923.)

We are not makers of these goods now.

BROOK'S ELEVATOR COMPANY.

(No. 1483.)

We have your report covering examination of our Royal mixed feed—No. 1483. Under head of microscopical examination we note you say it is composed of wheat product No. 1, corn cockle, and charlock. We are unable to account for this, owing to the fact we purchase the feed—composed of bran, middlings, and flour—direct from our large mills here in bulk, * * * and we aim to use only absolutely pure offal. * * *

Comment by authors.—A second examination was made and the same results obtained as at the first examination.

BUFFALO CEREAL COMPANY.

(Nos. 1583, 1954, 1573, 1523, 1541, 1972, 1582, 1625, 1741, 1922, 1598, 1792, 1554.)

We have the reports of your miscellaneous laboratory giving the analyses of feeds and by-products sold by our company, numbered 1583, 1954, 1573, 1523, 1541, 1972, 1582, 1625, 1741, 1922, 1598, 1792, 1554, and as we note that these results are to be published, we beg to take exception to the figures given, and in support of our exception we are inclosing a table. * * * In regard to the horse feed, the average of nine analyses, as given by the different States, shows that our feed was fully up to the guarantee given, * * * and in no case did the fat show as low as 3.30 or 4.11, as given by your Department.

In the case of dairy feed, * * * you will notice that the figures are considerably higher than yours.

In the case of creamery feed, 10 analyses show 19.95 per cent protein against 20 per cent guaranteed and 4.56 per cent fat against 5 per cent guaranteed, and in no case were there any samples that showed a figure as low as given in your 1972.

In regard to the poultry feed, the average of our three analyses is fairly close to the guarantee, but the fat as given under your 1582 is much too high. * * *

In regard to stock feed, we are also unable to find any analysis giving as low fat as those reported by you under your numbers 1741 and 1922.

In regard to hominy feed, you will also notice that in 12 analyses taken from the different bulletins we have no record of any fat determination running as low as your 1792.

Comment by authors.—All fat and protein determinations were repeated on the above samples. The figures for protein on Buffalo horse feed remained the same as before, while one fat figure on prolonged extraction rose above the guaranty.

The figures for both protein and fat in Buffalo creamery feed were slightly raised on repeating these determinations in sample No. 1972. In the other two samples of these feeds the figures remained unchanged.

The figures for both protein and fat remained the same in poultry feed (No. 1582) when these determinations were repeated.

The figures for protein on Buffalo XXX stock food (Nos. 1741, 1922) remained unchanged on a second examination, while the figures for fat were increased on a prolonged extraction, but not sufficiently to raise their samples above the guarantee of 4.50 per cent fat.

The figures for protein and fat on Buffalo hominy feed (No. 1792) were repeated and the same results obtained.

W. F. CHAMBERLAIN.

(No. 1915.)

* * * The analysis of our Perfect chick feed must have been made from an old lot, as we have not been using oyster shell for some time in our mixture. Our Perfect chick feed as we now put it up contains charcoal.

Comment by authors.—The sample collected in 1904 was again examined and oyster shells again found, but no charcoal.

CHAPIN & CO.

(Nos. 1614, 1789, 1843, 1515, 1708, 1722, 1797.)

Referring to your samples 1614, 1789, 1843, Ajax flakes, this brand of feed is now put out by the Ajax Milling and Feed Company, Buffalo, N. Y., and has been for the past year.

Referring to your samples 1515, 1708, 1722, 1797 (linseed-oil meal, O. P.) * * * as to the microscopical examination, the presence of weed seeds is accounted for only by the fact that in most oil mills the flaxseed screenings, consisting of light flax and various seeds, are screened before pressing the seed and these screenings are subsequently run into their meal in the case of many mills.

CYPHER'S INCUBATOR COMPANY.

(Nos. 1854, 1739, 1759, 1693, 1581, 1795, 1893.)

* * * In looking over these reports we can only come to the conclusion that there has been some radical mistake made in your reports or that you have gotten hold of products not of our manufacture, although possibly disguised under our name. We will take them up one at a time.

Cypher's clover meal (1854): We discontinued manufacturing clover meal early in the spring of 1904.

Cypher's chick food (1739): You state that you find it to contain mostly wheat screenings, also that you find foxtail, charlock, smartweed, chess, and rough pigweed in it, also rock. We beg to state that we positively have never put out a pound of chick food that contained an ounce of wheat screenings or wild seed of any kind. * * * It is possible that a year or more ago samples of our chick food may have been picked up that contained three pounds of chick grit in each 100 pounds of food. This was put in as a necessary element, but this year we omit it and caution the buyer that the grit must be supplied separately.

Cypher's forcing food (1759): * * * There is absolutely no weed seed and no wheat screenings.

Cypher's scratching food (1693): You report that you find it contains wheat product No. 2. * * * We beg to state that Cypher's scratching food is now and always has been made up of whole grains.

Cypher's laying food (1581, 1795, 1893): You have three reports of this product. In two of them you give wheat product No. 1, corn meal, and some animal meal as being the products which it is found to contain. You have overlooked altogether the product which is the base of our laying food and several others highly important for egg production that appear prominently in the other reports of laying food. * * * It contains no wheat screenings or seeds of smartweed, foxtail, or charlock.

Comment by authors.—Cypher's chick food (1739): The microscopist made a second examination of this product and found no reason to change his original findings.

Cypher's forcing food (1759): The microscopist made a second examination of this product and found no reason to change his findings, except in so far as to say that wheat screenings were not present in large quantities.

Cypher's scratching food (1693): The microscopist made a second examination and found more of the outside coats of grains than should be present in whole grains.

Cypher's laying food (1581, 1795, 1893): The microscopist made a second examination and was unable to find any products except those given in the table. There was no reason to change the findings in regard to weed seed.

DAYTON MILLING COMPANY.

(No. 1701.)

Referring to the analysis you have just sent us of No. 1701 (chop feed), in regard to the microscopical examination we are unable to tell what quality of our feed you analyzed. We make several qualities. One quality contains no whole oats and the other contains no oat hulls. * * * Any cockle or smartweed * * * came in with the oats and any buckwheat hulls are the product of the whole grain. This comes in either with the oats, which we buy locally, or is a slight mixture of the grain in going through the elevators.

D. A. DE LIMA & CO.

(No. 1521.)

* * * The microscopical examination, as you have it, is not correct, also the percentage of protein we guarantee is 12.5 per cent; fat 7.5 per cent * * * The fault we have to find with the microscopical examination of our Puritan chick food (1521) is that to the very best of our knowledge our food contains no oats.

Comment by authors.—The protein and fat determinations were repeated and the same results obtained. Oats were found only in traces, probably as a slight unintentional contamination.

EMPIRE MILLS.

(Nos. 1615, 1753.)

We can not understand how the ether extract is so low in either case of Empire feed (Nos. 1615, 1753). Would say our feed does not contain any pigweed or foul stuff of any kind. It is made from corn, hominy, and light oats and a very little barley * * * can not understand why there is so much difference in the moisture in these two cases. The analyses we have from different small stations have always given our feed as about 9 per cent protein and 3.5 to 4 per cent fat. Our guaranty is 7.63 per cent protein and 3.97 per cent fat.

Comment by authors.—The protein and fat determinations were repeated and the same results obtained. The microscopical examination was also repeated and the same results obtained. No barley could be found and pigweed was present in small quantities.

FALL CREEK MILLING COMPANY.

(No. 1713.)

Your analysis of No. 1713 ground corn and oats received. We grind corn and oat feed, sound grain, with no adulteration or filler. * * *

Comment by authors.—The microscopist repeated his work and obtained the same results as at the first examination.

GEORGE L. HARDING.

(Nos. 1711, 1930, 1556.)

I have your analysis of Harding's unexcelled baby chick food (1711, 1930) and egg building ration (1556). It is only fair to me that the analysis you make for publication be made on the mixture that I am placing on the market at the present time. Last year my mixture contained a certain per cent of ground grit, but this year that has been limited. * * * No. 1907, baby chick food mixture, contains nothing but dried milk cracked to chick size, wheat, corn, Kafir corn, and seeds, no screenings, no charcoal, no grit, or bone. The egg builder contains meat, bone, wheat, buckwheat, Kafir corn, millet, sunflower seed, beet seed, and corn.

Comment by authors.—The microscopist made a second examination of our sample of these goods and the substances reported in the table were found.

ALBERT A. KEENE.

(No. 1934.)

Referring to your copy of analysis of oat feed (1934), would say I have not put out any of this oat feed for six months or more and do not expect to do so in the future.

LAWRENCEBURG ROLLER MILL.

(Nos. 1597, 1919.)

We are in receipt of the analyses of our Snowflake and Golden Bull mixed feeds, Nos. 1597 and 1919. * * * Referring to Snowflake mixed feed * * * the words "middlings or shorts" [are used] and referring to Golden Bull the word "bran." Snowflake mixed feed is milled from soft winter wheat and Golden Bull mixed feed from hard spring wheat. Inasmuch as they both are the full run of offals, only the flour having been extracted, we do not understand these notations.

Comment by authors.—The microscopist made a second examination and obtained the same results as at his first examination, which would be expected, and with the manufacturer's explanation only goes to show how confused is the nomenclature of the by-products of flour manufacture.

THE MANN BROTHERS COMPANY.

(Nos. 1480, 1790, 1889.)

* * * There is an error so far as relates to smartweed seed [in our linseed meal 1480, 1790, 1889]. Our seed before crushing is cleaned as close as the most approved machinery can do it.

Comment by authors.—Another examination was made by the microscopist and smartweed seeds were found in small quantities.

MIDLAND LINSEED COMPANY.

(No. 1791.)

* * * The results of your analysis [of our ground oil cake 1791] are much poorer than reports of analyses of our oil cake by the various State experimental farms and we therefore believe that your report does not refer to samples of our oil cake or else you have not obtained fair samples.

Comment by authors.—The protein and fat determinations were repeated, and by prolonged extraction the fat was raised a slight amount.

MINER-HILLARD MILLING COMPANY.

(No. 1913.)

Referring to your analysis of hominy feed No. 1913, supposed to have been manufactured by us, will say that our mill was destroyed by fire early in the spring of 1904, consequently the sample you analyzed was not the product of our mill. While our plant was being rebuilt we purchased hominy feed from various western mills to fill our contracts, but always with the guaranty that it was to be up to our regular grades. * * *

Comment by authors.—The protein and fat determinations were repeated and the fat was raised by a prolonged extraction, but the protein remained the same.

HENRY. NEFF.

(No. 1699.)

In regard to examination of feed sample No. 1699 * * * I intend to mix one bushel of oats to a bushel of corn. The only way I can account for the excess of hulls and the low per cent of fat and proteids, same must have been taken when the bin was nearly empty * * *.

Comment by authors.—The fat and proteid determinations were repeated and the same results obtained.

ONEONTA MILLING COMPANY.

(Nos. 1496, 1510, 1704, 1572.)

We have your report No. 1510 * * * relating to analysis of our corn and oat provender. We note that microscopical examination shows rye, a trace of buckwheat hulls, etc. This we believe is not a fair sample of our corn and oat provender. We grind buckwheat at our mill, also rye, but neither of these products are intentionally included in our corn and oat provender. Our mill is equipped with spiral conveyors, and through the same conveyors we convey buckwheat, rye, corn, and oats, and also our provender.

It seems very probable to us that there has been unintentionally a mixture of the feed from which the sample was taken which you analyzed.

Comment by authors.—The microscopical examination was repeated and buckwheat and rye were found in small amounts.

* * * One sample, 1496 (arrow corn and oat feed), you report shows a trace of buckwheat hulls * * *. The trace of buckwheat in the feed is doubtless accounted for by buckwheat accumulating in our spiral conveyors * * *.

We also note your report No. 1704, reporting analysis of provender, which we note shows a trace of rough pigweed. * * * We can not account for its presence in the oat feed, which is used in mixing up this product * * *.

Sample 1572, * * * Monarch horse feed, * * * we discontinued making some time ago.

Comment by authors.—The microscopical examinations were repeated and the same results obtained.

R. C. RATHBORNE.

(No. 1820.)

* * * Your analysis 1820 (of chick meal) agrees very closely with our own. * * * You appear to have taken your sample for analysis from food sent out of this

factory over a year ago, or over two years ago, * * * for we have not mixed shells with it for many months. * * * The food is composed of meat and wheat flour * * *.

Comment by authors.—The microscopical examination was repeated and the results as given in the table obtained.

ROSS BROTHERS COMPANY.

(No. 1920.)

We have your notice of our Wyandotte chick food, No. 1920 * * *. In the list of articles you report as finding, we notice hulled oats, but no hulled oats are used in this feed; we use steel-cut oatmeal. The charlock and smartweed must be in the millet seed.

W. H. SMALL & CO.

(No. 1960.)

* * * What we fear is that you have obtained a sample of an old chicken-feed mixture (No. 1960) that we formerly put out, but which has been abandoned for at least a year.

J. E. SOPER & CO.

(No. 1852.)

We have your report No. 1852 giving analysis of our brand of Blue Ribbon hominy feed. * * * Upon receipt of your report we took the matter up with the manufacturers, calling their attention to the low fat analysis, * * * and we quote from their letter * * *:

"The Government report on hominy which you inclose certainly does seem low in the amount of fat. * * * We do not remember any analysis that has given such a low per cent of fat * * *." -

Comment by authors.—The results on fat and protein were repeated, and higher results were obtained on fat by a prolonged extraction.

SPARKS MILLING COMPANY.

(Nos. 1501, 1543.)

We have received this morning the chemical and microscopical analyses of two of our feeds, Nos. 1501 and 1543, Tri-me mixed feed * * *: The Tri-me mixed feed is composed of pure wheat bran and middlings. * * * If there is any smartweed seed in the feed, it is evidently a very small proportion, as it could only be what was mixed in with the wheat when it reached us direct from the farms. The same applies to the bran, chess, and yellow dock seed in sample 1543. * * *

Comment by authors.—Another microscopical examination was made and the same weed seeds found, but they were present in very small quantities.

DAVID STOTT.

(Nos. 1619, 1509, 1989.)

Replying to your circular letter regarding samples of my feed, Nos. 1619, 1509, 1989, I think especially your remarks under the head of "Microscopical examination" are misleading. You probably recognize that the articles other than pure bran or middlings are impossible to separate from the wheat in the condition in which it is usually purchased. These are such a small portion of the feed that they should be specified as ground screenings or something to indicate that they are not deliberately added or in any quantity present in the feed.

Comment by authors.—The manufacturer was informed that the weed seeds were only found in small amounts.

SWIFT & CO.

(No. 1773.)

* * * Regarding Swift's blood meal; On the basis of 8 per cent moisture, blood meal will uniformly show 87 per cent protein, instead of 85.56 per cent shown as result of your analysis No. 1773.

THORNTON & CHESTER MILLING COMPANY.

(No. 1473, 1779.)

* * * Our mixed feed (1473, 1779), which your Department has sampled and analyzed, is the entire feed product from the wheat, and so includes what is known in the trade as bran, shorts, and middlings.

Comment by authors.—The microscopical examination was repeated, and it was found that the sample consisted so largely of the outer seed coats that it was necessary to classify it as wheat product No. 1.

UNION LINSEED COMPANY.

(No. 1586.)

In reply to yours of recent date giving an analysis of linseed-oilmeal "cow" (1586), would state that our plant was destroyed by fire over a year ago, and that we have been out of business since that time, and have no intention of resuming. * * *

THE UNITED STATES FRUMENTUM COMPANY.

(No. 1758.)

* * * The analysis of our frumentum hominy feed (1758) as to fat and protein shows a higher per cent than your statement. A recent analysis of our feed shows protein 11.37 per cent and fat 9.25 per cent, which is a fair average. * * *

Comment by authors.—The determinations of fat and protein were repeated and the same results obtained.

A. WALKER & CO.

(No. 1478.)

Yours received advising us of analysis of our Blue Grass mixed feed (1478). We note the result of this analysis shows somewhat below what we are claiming for it. We arrived at this analysis by sending standard samples to several different chemists, and thought we were perfectly safe in guaranteeing our feed to show 11 per cent protein and 3 per cent fat. * * *

Comment by authors.—Protein and fat determinations were repeated and the same results obtained.

E. S. WOODWORTH & CO.

(Nos. 1604, 1933, and 1958.)

We are in receipt of your analyses of "00" yellow and "00" white feed (1604, 1933, and 1958), manufactured by the Diamond Elevator and Milling Company. * * * We beg to call your attention to the fact that the Diamond Elevator and Milling Company as a corporation no longer exists. We own and operate the Diamond Mill and Elevator, and all feeds will now go out under our name and brands. It is not likely that we will manufacture any more of the "00" feeds. If we do, however, we will take pains to have them entirely up to our guaranteed analyses. * * *

MICROSCOPICAL EXAMINATION.

By B. J. Howard,

Chief, Microchemical Laboratory.

GENERAL REMARKS.

The microscopical examination of the stock foods offers more complicated features than that of human foods because of the contaminations which are commonly present. These are due to one or more of three causes: (1) The use of screenings and other by-products; (2) the use of low-grade grains containing more or less weed seed; and (3) the willful addition of foreign matter as a makeweight. The results obtained in the investigation indicate that the last named is the least common form of adulteration.

The wide diversity of materials which are used in stock foods and which are susceptible of microscopic detection, as well as the vast array of weed seeds which may be present to greater or less extent, offers for the microscopist a wide field if he is to treat the subject comprehensively.

The literature upon the microscopic examination of human foods and drugs covers part of the field; but there is no publication upon this subject alone, either original or compiled data, in convenient form for the average worker. To cover the field fully would be impracticable in a report of this nature, but it seems important to give some attention to the structure of the principal ingredients and the most important of the weed seeds which have been observed. Most of the weed seeds may in small quantities be considered harmless to stock, but a few are sufficiently poisonous when present in considerable amounts to produce serious results. To this last class belong seeds of the jimson weed (*Datura stramonium* L.), corn cockle (*Agrostemma githago* L.), and darnel (*Lolium temulentum* L.).

APPARATUS, REAGENTS, AND METHODS.

The methods used in performing this work are for the most part simple in their technique. The apparatus consists first of a suitable microscope giving a magnification of from 75 or 90 for the low power up to a combination giving at least 200.

It was rarely found necessary to exceed this, though some workers prefer somewhat higher power. A supply of microscope slides of

72

regulation size, namely, 25 mm x 75 mm, and cover glasses are required. The round form covers of 18 mm diameter (¾-inch) and 0.17 mm to 0.25 mm in thickness were preferred, because they are less easily broken in cleaning than the square ones. Scalpels, tearing needles, and a small alcohol lamp or a gas microburner are also needed.

The most important reagents used are as follows: Distilled water, alcohol, dilute glycerin (glycerin water 1 : 1), iodin in potassium iodid solution, dilute hydrochloric acid (strong acid and water 1 : 2), and chloral hydrate solution (chloral hydrate crystals 8 parts, water 5 parts).

As a clearing agent chloral hydrate was used almost exclusively, and for all except the very densest brown or black seed coats it is perfectly satisfactory, while even with the darkest colored seeds it can be used with fairly good results if the heating is sufficiently prolonged. To make use of the reagent a portion of the sample is placed on a slide with a few drops of the chloral hydrate solution and heated to boiling for a few moments. This dissolves the starch and has a general clearing action so that the structure can be more clearly seen. If the solution boils away before the clearing is completed more should be added, as the specimen should not be allowed to become dry during the process. With very refractory specimens a small amount of nitric acid is sometimes added, but this reagent must be used with care since it attacks the tissues so vigorously. Some workers recommend caustic alkali, but this requires some little time to act, and Javelle water (chlorinated potash) is open to the same objection.

LIST OF MATERIALS THAT MAY BE PRESENT IN CATTLE FOODS.

It is not intended at this time to go extensively into the histological features of the constituents of stock foods. In the following list are given the materials which have been reported in stock foods, more or less frequently, by various observers.[a]

CEREAL PRODUCTS.

The most important constituents in the list are the cereal grains, such as wheat, barley, rye, corn, oats, rice, and their by-products from milling processes.

---

[a] Street, Report of New Jersey Agricultural Experiment Station, 1905; Bul. No. 117, Inland Revenue Department, Ottawa, Canada; Winton, Microscopy of Vegetable Foods; Maryland Agricultural College Quarterly, May, 1907; Tirsch and Oesterle, Anatomischer Atlas der Pharmakognosie und Nahrungsmittelkunde, 1893–1900; Conn. Exper. Stat. bulletins, especially No. 132.

Of the wheat products there are three, designated in Table 2 as W. P. No. 1, W. P. No. 2, and W. P. No. 3.   These abbreviations have the following significance:

Wheat product No. 1: Composed mostly of the outer seed coats (pericarp) of the wheat kernel.   In addition there are small amounts of the other seed coats, aleuron layer, endosperm (starchy portions), and germ.

Wheat product No. 2: Composed of relatively less of the pericarp and of a greater portion of the inner coats, aleuron layer, germ, and a considerably larger amount of the endosperm in more or less broken condition.   The portions of epicarp present are usually of smaller size than those of wheat product No. 1.

Wheat product No. 3: Composed mostly of the inner seed coats, aleuron layer, and starchy portions with a small amount of the epicarp, and sometimes small amounts of germ.   The most important difference between this and product No. 2 is that there is a larger amount of endospermous material.

SECONDARY OR BY-PRODUCTS.

After the cereal products should be mentioned the following:

Linseed and linseed meal.
Cottonseed meal.
Millet.
Kaffir corn, Guinea corn, sorghum, broom corn, durra (*Andropogon sorghum* var).
Corncobs, with or without the corn.
Malt sprouts.
Brewers' grains (barley, oats, corn, etc., residues).
Distillers' grains (corn, rye, barley, oat, etc., residues).
Glucose by-products (commonly composed of changed corn starch and germ).
Sunflower seed.
Clover-seed chaff.
Dried sugar-beet pulp.
Buckwheat hulls.
Peanut hulls.
Peas and pea hulls.
Animal meal (muscle tissue, tankage, etc.).
Armenian bole (red clay of Armenia).
Bone meal.
Cocoa hulls.
Dried blood.
Ground rock.
Ground shells (oyster, clam, etc.).
Sand.

WEED SEEDS.

The following are the most important of the weed seeds found in stock food:

Corn cockle (*Agrostemma githago* L.; *Lychnis githago* Scop.).
Black bindweed, wild buckwheat (*Polygonum convolvulus* L.).
Smartweed (*Polygonum hydropiper* L.).

Lady's thumb, smartweed (*Polygonum persicaria* L.).

Curled dock seed (*Rumex crispus* L.).

Sorrel (*Rumex acetosella* L.).

Cow cockle, cow-herb (*Vaccaria vaccaria* (L.) Britton; *Vaccaria vulgaris* Host; *Saponaria vaccaria* L.).

Soapwort, Bouncing Bet (*Saponaria officinalis* L.).

Charlock, wild mustard, Dakota mustard (*Brassica arvensis* (L.) B. S. P.; *Brassica sinapistrum* Boiss; *Sinapis arvensis* L.), and other species.

Darnel, tares (*Lolium temulentum* L.).

Jimson weed, Jamestown weed, thorn apple (*Datura stramonium* L.).

Pigweed (*Chenopodium* sp.).

Rough pigweed (*Amaranthus* sp.).

Green foxtail (*Chaetochloa viridis* (L.) Scribn.; *Setaria viridis* Beauv.).

Yellow foxtail (*Chaetochloa glauca* (L.) Scribn.; *Setaria glauca* Beauv.).

Bracted plantain (*Plantago aristata* Michx.), erroneously called buckhorn.

Rib grass (*P. lanceolata* L.).

Rugel's plantain (*P. rugelii* Decaisne).

Chess (*Bromus secalinus* L.).

Rose seed (*Rosa* sp.).

Pepper grass (*Lepidium virginicum* L.).

Hare's-ear (*Conringia orientalis* (L.) Dumort).

Ragweed (*Ambrosia artemisiæfolia* L.).

Night-flowering catchfly (*Silene noctiflora* L.).

Wild bergamot, horse mint (*Monarda fistulosa* L.).

The materials entering into stock foods are of such character that the presence of weed seeds to a greater or less extent is almost universal in certain kinds—for example, in oats. As every one is aware who is familiar with this grain there is often present quite a large amount of pigweed as well as other seeds. In preparing stock feed there is commonly little or no attempt made to remove such foreign material and so it will usually appear in the final product. In this report there are mentioned by name, as far as possible, all those cases where weed seeds have been found, but in most cases such presence should not cause the product to be condemned, since the microscopic method will often detect and identify them when the quantity present would not in the least affect the value of the product. In the case of poisonous seeds, however, the amount should of course be kept at a minimum, for if present to any extent the product becomes positively injurious.

As an illustration of this might be mentioned a case of the poisoning of poultry by corn cockle which recently came to the writer's attention. Although this seed is rarely considered poisonous, yet in sufficient amounts it is very harmful. Corn cockle [a] is a frequent weed contamination in wheat and is usually present in such small amounts that no notice is taken of it, but in the case referred to a large number of chickens had been killed. The owners attributed the trouble to the wheat middlings which they were feeding. An examination for metallic poisons was first made, but none was found. A microscopic examination of the food, however, showed that there

---

[a] Chesnut, U. S. Dept. Agr., Farmers' Bulletin No. 86.

was a large amount of corn cockle present—a much larger amount than was found in any samples here reported. Other seeds which are more or less poisonous are the jimson weed (*Datura stramonium* L.) and the darnel (*Lolium temulentum* L.). Fortunately the corn cockle and jimson weed have very characteristic structures, by which they can be readily identified, even though well ground.

Special acknowledgments are due to Mr. F. H. Hillman and Dr. C. F. Wheeler, of the Bureau of Plant Industry, who furnished a standard collection of weed seeds of known identity for use in making this study.

MEDICINAL OR CONDIMENTAL MATERIALS.

Substances of medicinal or condimental character which are sometimes found are as follows:

OF VEGETABLE ORIGIN.

Anise.
Asafetida.
Bayberry bark.
Black pepper.
Blood root.
Carob bean (St. John's bread).
Capsicum.
Coriander seed.
Elecampane.
Fennel.
Fenugrec.
Gentian root.

Ginger.
Hemp.
Juniper berries.
Licorice root.
Lobelia.
Mandrake.
Oak bark.
Poplar bark.
Senna.
Turmeric.
Valerian.
Walnut bark.

OF MINERAL ORIGIN.

Alum.
Antimony.
Arsenic.
Calcium carbonate.
Calcium phosphate.
Charcoal.
Coperas.
Iron oxid.

Potassium nitrate (saltpeter)
Rosin.
Salt, common.
Salts, Glauber's.
Salts, Epsom.
Sodium carbonate.
Sulphur.

HISTOLOGICAL FEATURES OF SOME CATTLE-FOOD CONSTITUENTS.

A description of the histological features of some of the most common ingredients of cattle foods, and also of some of the more important of our common weed seeds, is given in the following discussion. Many others, such as corn, barley, oats, etc., are not discussed, as they are amply treated in the literature of the subject.

WHEAT AND RYE.

In products containing seed coats of these grains the histological features of the cross cells are sufficient to identify them. These cells

Four features of the cottonseed deserve attention. The first three of these are found in the seed coverings. The outer layer of the seed coat consists of very irregular but usually somewhat elongated cells, which are very characteristic of cottonseed. (Plate II, fig. 1.) They are of light to rather deep brown color.

The second coat, occasionally found, is the layer of palisade cells. (Plate II, fig. 2). In the surface view they have an irregular honeycombed appearance, and commonly crossing each cell are to be found a few lines more or less parallel.

The third layer of note is the delicate membrane (perisperm) enwrapping the embryo, and this looks like a network, with somewhat indefinite outlines. (Plate II, fig. 3.)

If none of the foregoing structures was present it might be difficult to identify cottonseed meal, though in the embryo there occur numerous small rosette crystals of calcium oxalate, which are strongly indicative of cottonseed. They will be found embedded in fragments of the embryo, which, after clearing, have a bright light-yellow color and which, with the small crystals, are not likely to be confused with other structures that may be present in this class of cattle foods.

LINSEED (FLAX).

There are two structures of the linseed that are characteristic. The first of these is a layer composed of long sclerenchymatous cells of straw color. The pits in the walls give them a faint beaded appearance. (Plate II, fig. 5.)

The second layer of importance, from a diagnostic point of view, are the quadratic pigment cells. (Plate II, fig. 6.) These cells are commonly nearly square or polygonal, with nearly clear walls, but containing brown-colored contents. In the walls are numerous fine pits.

CAROB BEAN.

The pods of this fruit are sometimes used in cattle foods, and when so used in a ground condition can be most easily identified by the appearance and reactions of the tannin cells. While in a growing condition the contents of these cells are fluid and give a strong tannin reaction with iron chlorid solution. When ripe, however, the contents become solid and of a dark amber color, and though slow in giving the tannin reaction finally produce a pronounced black color. Winton recommends the use of dilute alkali, which, in the cold, colors the bodies green, changing to blue-gray, while heating produces a violet color.

ANIMAL MEAL.

The presence of this substance can be easily established by the presence of striated muscle fibers, which are easily identified after clearing the material with chloral hydrate and stopping down the microscope substage diaphragm.

BONE MEAL.

This substance is identified by the characteristic lacunæ and canaliculi, which occur abundantly in bone tissue and which are readily visible in material that has been cleared. (Plate III, fig. 4.)

OYSTER AND CLAM SHELLS.

To the naked eye fragments of these have a bright, shiny appearance. Under the microscope they show no lacunæ or canaliculi, and with dilute hydrochloric acid give a more vigorous effervescence than bone meal.

DRIED BLOOD.

This material has the appearance of a black powder or meal. The best way to establish the identity of this substance is by the hematin test. The method used has been to mount some of the material to be tested on a slide with a few drops of water to which has been added one or two tiny crystals of sodium chlorid. It is allowed to stand until nearly dry, and then, after covering, a few drops of glacial acetic acid are added and heated on a steam bath or hot radiator or over the micro-burner for two to five minutes, adding more acid from time to time if required. Finally the slide is removed and allowed to slowly cool. If the test has been properly conducted the presence of blood will be shown by the presence of small plate crystals. (Plate III, fig. 3.) In order to obtain crystals of good size, the final cooling must be conducted slowly.

CHARLOCK, WILD MUSTARD.

Brassica arvensis (L.) B. S. P.

This weed is a frequent contamination of grains, and to a casual observer the entire seed looks like black mustard seed, though a comparison will show the charlock to be slightly larger, plumper, and usually of darker color.

When ground, the seed coats show the characteristic palisade cells common to the Brassica family. (Plate I, fig. 1.) A distinguishing test, however, has been observed in its reaction toward chloral hydrate solution. When boiled with this reagent, as is done in clearing for microscopical examination, a deep crimson color is developed, which has not been noted for other species of this genus.

COMMON PIGWEED.

Chenopodium sp.

The seeds of the two common species are much alike in size and shape, the *C. album* L. being possibly a little the smaller. To the akene, as commonly found, more or less of the dried floral envelope is attached. The seeds are nearly in the form of biconvex lenses and have a diameter of $\frac{2}{3}$ to $1\frac{1}{4}$ mm. Those of *C. album* L. have a somewhat glossy surface while those of *C. murale* L. have a dull surface.

In color and resistance to clearing, the seed coats of this species resemble strongly those of rough pigweed. A microscopic examination reveals a surface composed of cells more or less rectangular or rounded in outline and of about 30 μ to 75 μ in longest diameter, with somewhat rounded corners. (Plate I, fig. 5.) The surfaces of the cells are covered with papilla-like projections, giving a dotted or punctate appearance.

ROUGH PIGWEED.

Amaranthus sp.

The seeds of *A. blitoides* S. Wats., *A. hybridus* L., *A. retroflexus* L., and *A. albus* L. are flattened seeds with a very glossy black surface (brown in seeds not perfectly ripe). In size the *A. blitoides* is the largest, being about 1 to $1\frac{1}{4}$ mm in diameter; *A. albus* is the smallest, about $\frac{1}{2}$ mm. The seeds of *A. hybridus* vary in size from $\frac{2}{3}$ to 1 mm, and are slightly elongated into ovate form. The same may be said of *A. retroflexus*, though in size the seeds are intermediate between *A. hybridus* and *A. albus*.

· The coats of this seed are dark brown in color and when cleared sufficiently are found to present in surface view a mosaic work of polygonal cells of approximately six sides. The cells are of about 17 μ to 35 μ in diameter. (Plate I, fig. 6.) The limits of the cells are defined by a sharp, fine line. The surface of the cells are covered thickly by fine dots, giving almost a punctate appearance.

BINDWEED, SMARTWEED.

Polygonum sp.

The seeds of *P. convolvulus* L. have the form of buckwheat grains, being about 3 to 3.5 mm long, and of a dull, coal-black color. *P. pennsylvanicum* L. has flat seeds 3 to 3.5 mm long, of shiny brown color. The seeds of *P. persicaria* L. are about 1 to 1.25 mm long, generally flat, though occasionally buckwheat-shaped specimens are found, and of a shiny deep brown or black color. *P. hydropiper* L. seeds are of buckwheat shape, like *P. convolvulus*, but of smaller size (2.5 to 3 mm) and of dull light to dark brown color.

The seed coats of the members of the genus *Polygonum persicaria* are commonly so deep brown in color that considerable boiling is frequently required to clear them sufficiently for examination. When satisfactory clearing has been accomplished the surface of *P. persicaria* is found to have a dotted appearance, the dots being arranged somewhat in rows. If the specimen is sufficiently cleared the pits can usually be seen as fine lines radiating through the clearer portion of the walls between the dots or holes, which in reality are holes in the epidermal cells. (Plate VI, fig. 5.)

WILD BERGAMOT.

Monarda fistulosa L.

These seeds are pale to dark drab in color, 1.5 to 1.75 mm in length by about 1 mm wide; one side is curved, while the other is compressed into a ridge near the base, which is more or less common in the mint family.

The seed coats are characteristic. The epidermal cells have thick walls of very strongly convoluted outline. (Plate II, fig. 4.) The inner part of the coat is lined with a layer of thin-walled rectangular cells, the walls of which have a beading which is more pronounced near the hilum of the seed. The perisperm is a layer of delicate cells covering the endosperm and having quite strongly beaded walls. Embedded near the middle of the seed coats, at fairly regular intervals, are small black dots of spherical form, which appear plainly in either the surface or inner view of well-cleared fragments of the seed coats and also in cross sections. By continued boiling with chloral hydrate they may be bleached so as to be almost invisible. Examination of other plants of the mint family indicates that these dots occur in other genera also, for example in *Hedeoma pulegioides* Pers.

COW HERB.

Vaccaria vaccaria (L.) Britton.

The seeds of this weed are blue black in color, nearly spherical in shape, and about 2 mm in diameter. To the naked eye the surface has a slightly dull appearance. Microscopically the seed coats are very characteristic. The epidermal cells are polygonal in shape, and the walls have saw-tooth outlines, the teeth having a length equal to about one-third of the cell diameter. (Plate IV, fig. 1.) They resemble the cells of the *Saponaria officinalis* L., but are more regular in outline and not so large, though the thickness of the walls is somewhat greater. The middle lamella in well-cleaned material often appears as a dark line in the middle of the cell walls. The second layer of importance is one consisting of rectangular cells with nearly clear walls, but brown contents. (Plate IV, fig. 2.) They are found on the inner side of the seed coats near the hilum and extend for a short distance over the radicle. They recall in appearance quite strongly the pigment cells of flaxseed, but are not so regular and are smaller, though with thicker walls and coarser pits.

JIMSON WEED.

Datura stramonium L.

The seeds of jimson weed are like the lima bean in shape, 3 to 3.75 mm in length, and of a dark brown or black color. The surface is covered with small depressions, giving a rough appearance to the seed.

These examinations lead to the conclusion that fortunately this poisonous seed is not often found in cattle foods. Its identification is a simple matter, for the seed coats have very characteristic markings. The coats consist of cells of very sinuous outlines, the indentations often extending nearly to the center of the cells. (Plate IV, fig. 4.) The walls are highly refractive to light, and though quite easily cleared are difficult to represent very satisfactorily in a photograph.

PLANTAIN.

The structure of the various species of plantains is much alike, though it is possible to identify them. The seeds in general resemble miniature canoes, although in the case of *Plantago major* L. both sides of the seed are somewhat convex.

One interesting difference between the species is in the position of the cotyledons in the seed. In some of them the cotyledons are placed ventrally and dorsally, while in others they occupy a right-and-left position.

The leading characteristics of the four species which are quite frequently found in stock foods are as follows:

BRACTED PLANTAIN.

Plantago aristata Michx.

The seeds of this species are from 2 to 3 mm in length and about half as wide, of a medium brown color, and have a dull surface. At the middle there crosses the seed transversely a slight depression readily seen with a hand lens.

The surface of the seeds is covered with mucilage cells which swell in water or aqueous solutions, and take on a characteristic hour-glass form. (Plate VI, fig. 1.) The endosperm cells are thick walled and have no pits in them. (Plate VI, fig. 2.) The position of the cotyledons is of the right-and-left type. (Plate V, fig. 4.)

RIB GRASS.

Plantago lanceolata L.

These seeds are of about the same size as those of *P. aristata* Michx., but have a bright brown to black color and no transverse depression.

The surface of the seeds of this species is smooth, and has very little of the mucilage layer found in *P. major* L. and *P. rugelii* Decaisne. After being mounted in water or chloral hydrate the endosperm cells swell and show prominent pits in their walls. The cotyledons have the right-and-left position in the seed. (Plate V, fig. 3.)

COMMON PLANTAIN.

Plantago major L.

Seeds vary from 1 to 1.5 mm in length, and are about two-thirds as wide; they are brown to black in color. These seeds are convex on both sides, not having the canoe shape which is characteristic of the other species studied. (Plate V, fig. 1.) The surface is covered with an outer very uneven layer of thin-walled cells. They are rather long, rectangular in form, and with quite uniformly wavy walls. (Plate VI, fig. 3.) They are arranged in rows with the long sides of the cells adjacent and at the ends where adjacent rows abut there is usually produced a ridge which, until well cleared, appears as a dark band. The endosperm cells show no beading in their walls. The cotyledons have a dorsal and ventral position in the seed.

RUGEL'S PLANTAIN.

Plantago rugelii Decaisne.

These seeds vary in size from 1.25 to 2 mm and are of a deep-brown or black color.

In some respects they resemble more clearly *P. major* than any of the others which we have studied. The cotyledons have the ventral and dorsal position in the seed (Plate V, fig. 2). The epidermal layer (Plate VI, fig. 4) consists of rectangular cells shorter than those of *P. major*, and, though they commonly are arranged in rows, they are rarely found to be continuous for more than eight or ten cells together, and the rows are not regularly parallel as in *P. major*.

CORN COCKLE.

Agrostemma githago L.

These seeds are crudely tetragonal in form and about 2.5 mm in diameter, of a dull deep-brown or black color, and are covered with a prominent papilla-like surface.

The papillæ are seen under the microscope to be provided with a projection from each of the epidermal cells. (Plate IV, fig. 3.) The cells are very characteristic, have sinuous outlines, and interlock with adjacent cells. Beside the large papillæ there are on the surface of the cells fine warty processes, readily seen under a magnification of 100.

BOUNCING BET.

Saponaria officinalis L.

These seeds are disk shaped somewhat like the lima bean, a dull, deep black color, and are about 2 mm in diameter. With a hand lens they are seen to have a papilla-like surface.

The seed coats resemble, in some respects, *Silene noctiflora* L. in the shape of the epidermal cells, but without the papilla-like projections or fine warty points (Plate IV, fig. 5), and the outlines of the cells are not as prominent.

NIGHT-FLOWERING CATCHFLY.

Silene noctiflora L.

These seeds are somewhat like tiny peas or shortened beans of about 1 mm diameter and of a dull gray color.

The seed coats of this species are highly characteristic (Plate IV, fig. 6), each cell having a saw-toothed outline interlocking with its neighbor. The middle lamella, constituting the bounding area, is highly refractive toward light. In the center of each cell is a dark portion produced by a protuberance forming a papilla-like roughness on the surface of the seed; between these large points are fine warty points, which, under the microscope, give it a slightly roughened appearance.

CURLED DOCK.

Rumex crispus L.

These seeds are the shape of buckwheat seeds, having three faces and pointed at both ends, though more obtusely at the base. In length they vary from 1.5 to 2 mm and are of a shiny brown color.

In the coats of this seed the cells have strongly sinuous outlines. (Plate VI, fig. 6.) The indentations are frequently half as great as the small diameter of the cells. Difficulty is sometimes experienced in sufficiently clearing these seed coats to enable one to see the markings well.

SORREL.

Rumex acetosella L.

These seeds in general shape are like those of *R. crispus* L. (p. 83) but are 1.25 to 1.50 mm in length, of a dull brown color, and have a somewhat roughened surface.

The sorrel seed coats are readily split into two ovate-shaped halves. Cleared and examined under the microscope, the surface will be found to be covered with strongly convoluted ridges, which are more or less parallel from end to end. (Plate III, fig. 1.)

FOXTAIL.

Chaetochloa sp.

The seeds of *C. glauca* (L.) Scribn. are about 3 mm by 2 mm, strongly flattened on the palet side, and of a dull greenish yellow color. The seeds of green foxtail *C. viridis* (L.) Scribn. are the shape of *C. glauca* but with a more convex palet and about one-half to two-thirds the dimensions. In color they vary from pale green to brown.

The principal structures for identification of the foxtails are the glumes and palets, and in a ground condition it seems rather difficult to differentiate *Chaetochloa glauca* from *Chaetochloa viridis*. The ridges on *C. glauca* usually can be seen in material which has been partially cleared in chloral hydrate, while in *C. viridis* (Plate III, fig. 2) most of the epidermal cells form projections which in the case of the palet are especially characteristic, and a careful examination of these two features will usually enable the worker to identify the two species.

INDEX TO PLATES.

85

PLATE VI.

Fig. 1. Slime cells from seed of *Plantago aristata* Michx.   ×75.
    2. Endosperm cells of seed of *P. aristata* Michx.   (The slime cells are out of focus and appear as hazy areas.)   ×150.
    3. Epidermal layer from *P. major* L.   ×150.
    4. Epidermal layer of *P. rugelii* Decaisne.   ×150.
    5. Surface view of epidermal layer of seed coat of smartweed (*Polygonum persicaria* L.).   ×150.
    6. Surface view of seed coat of curled dock (*Rumex crispus* L.).   ×150.

FIG. 1.—SEED COAT OF CHARLOCK.
(X 150.)

FIG. 2.—CROSS CELLS OF SEED COAT OF RYE.
(X 150.)

FIG. 3.—CROSS CELLS OF SEED COAT OF WHEAT.
(X 150.)

FIG. 4.—ALEURON LAYER OF WHEAT.
(X 150.)

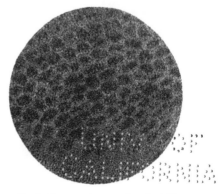

FIG. 5.—EPIDERMAL LAYER OF SEED COAT OF
COMMON PIGWEED. (X 150.)

FIG. 6.—EPIDERMAL LAYER OF SEED COAT OF
ROUGH PIGWEED. (X 150.)

FIG. 1.—EPIDERMAL LAYER OF SEED COAT OF
COTTON SEED. (X 75.)

FIG. 2.—PALISADE LAYER OF SEED COAT OF
COTTON SEED. (X 75.)

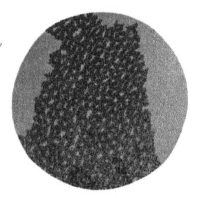

FIG. 3.—PERISPERM LAYER OF SEED COAT OF
COTTON SEED. (X 150.)

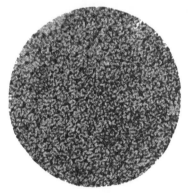

FIG. 4.—SEED COAT OF WILD BERGAMOT.
(X 150.)

FIG. 5.—SCLERENCHYMATOUS CELLS FROM SEED
COAT OF FLAXSEED. (X 150.)

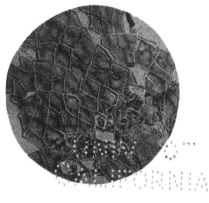

FIG. 6.—PIGMENT CELLS OF FLAXSEED.
(X 150.)

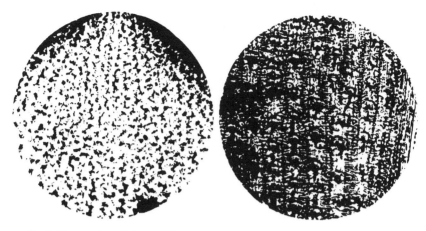

FIG. 1.—EPIDERMAL LAYER OF SORREL SEED
(X 150.)

FIG. 2.—EPIDERMAL LAYER OF GLUME OF
YELLOW FOXTAIL. (X 150.)

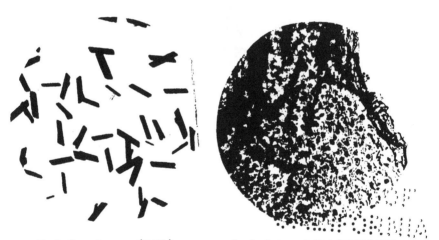

FIG. 3.—HEMIN CRYSTALS. (X 600.)

FIG. 4.—FRAGMENT OF BONE SHOWING LACUNÆ.

FIG. 1.—EPIDERMAL LAYER OF SEED COAT OF COW HERB. (X 150.)

FIG. 2.—BEADED CELLS NEAR HILUM OF SEED OF COW HERB. (X 300.)

FIG. 3.—EPIDERMAL CELLS OF CORN COCKLE. (X 75.)

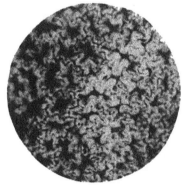

FIG. 4.—EPIDERMAL CELLS OF JIMSON WEED SEED. (X 75.)

FIG. 5.—EPIDERMAL CELLS OF SEEDS OF BOUNCING BET. (X 150.)

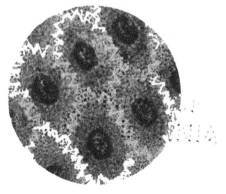

FIG. 6.—EPIDERMAL CELLS OF SEEG OF NIGHT-BLOOMING CATCHFLY. (X 150.)

Bul. 108, Bureau of Chemistry. U. S. Dept. of Agriculture.

PLATE V.

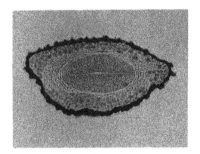

Fig. 1.—Plantago Major L.

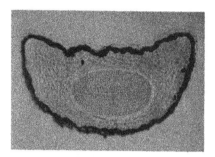

Fig. 2.—Plantago Rugelii Ducaisne.

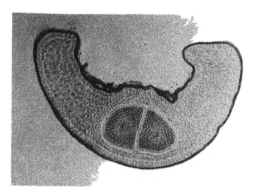

Fig. 3.—Plantago Lanceolata L.

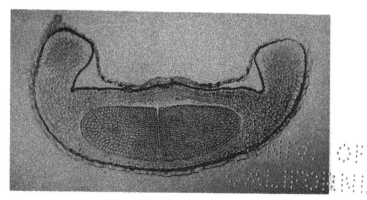

Fig. 4.—Plantago Aristata Michx.

TRANSVERSE SECTIONS OF SEEDS OF SPECIES OF GENUS PLANTAGO. (X 50.)

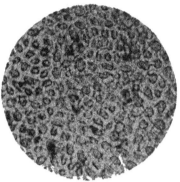

FIG. 1.—SLIME CELLS FROM SEED OF PLANTAGO
ARISTATA MICHX. (X 75.)

FIG. 2.—ENDOSPERM CELLS OF SEED OF PLANTAGO
ARISTATA MICHX. (X 150.)

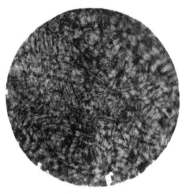

FIG. 3.—EPIDERMAL LAYER OF SEED OF PLANTAGO
MAJOR L. (X 150.)

FIG. 4.—EPIDERMAL LAYER OF SEED OF PLANTAGO
RUGELII DUCAISNE. (X 150.)

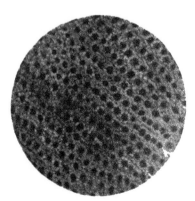

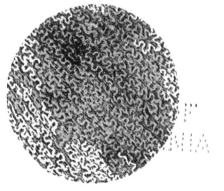

FIG. 5.—EPIDERMAL LAYER OF SEED COAT OF
SMARTWEED. (X 150.)

FIG. 6.—SEED COAT OF CURLED DOCK.
(X 150.)

ALPHABETICAL INDEX TO SAMPLES.

A.

B.

C.

<h3 style="text-align:center">H.</h3>

P.

Q.

R.

S.

O

RETURN
TO ➡

CIRCULATION DEPARTMENT
202 Main Library

LOAN PERIOD 1 **HOME USE**	2	3
4	5	6

ALL BOOKS MAY BE RECALLED AFTER 7 DAYS
1-month loans may be renewed by calling 642-3405
6-month loans may be recharged by bringing books to Circulation Desk
Renewals and recharges may be made 4 days prior to due date

DUE AS STAMPED BELOW

~~NECEIVER~~	FEB 06 1996	
NOV 15 1995		
	RECEIVED	
REC. CIR. MAY 1 '72	OCT 3 1 1996	
DEC 8 1979	CIRCULATION DEPT.	
REC. CIR. NOV 1 4 1979 NOV 3 0 1981		
REC'D DEC 2 1981		
DEC 1 1 1982		
REC. CIR. DEC 07 '82		

FORM NO. DD 6, 40m 10'77